To all those who have loved us,
and to all those we have loved.

Contents

Becoming aware of special gifts, "coincidences" or unexpected happenings, favors, intuitive messages, surprise calls
or encounters, special connections, magical intervention,
inspirations and out-of-the-blue information that shows up at
just the right time.

Noticing and valuing beauty in the environment; appreciating
textures, colors and sounds in nature; acknowledging visual
and sensory abundance.

Noticing and remembering images or messages from dreams,
daydreams, meditation, reflection, trances or déjà vu experiences; valuing thoughts, inspirations, imagination and gut feelings; listening.

Valuing the functionality, usefulness, convenience, beauty and
abundance of material possessions at home and at work; recognizing choices and prosperity.

Acknowledgments

*A*fter finishing the first, very rough draft of this book, we sent copies to a diverse group of friends, family members, colleagues and associates, asking them for their feedback and suggestions, and their reactions to everything from the chapter titles to the content and activities. We would like to gratefully acknowledge those special individuals who took the extra time to thoroughly go through this material and challenge us to rethink certain linguistic or conceptual choices we had made, and who caused us to take many of our initial ideas far beyond our original presentation. Their input helped this book develop more fully, and we feel that it is richer and more inspired because of their insightful contributions. Thank-yous to Lynn Collins, Morgan Daleo, Mary Ann Dockstader, Cinda Fairfield, Dave Friedli, Rick Harter, Dave Hinckley, Marcia Kons, Nicholas Mann, Sandi Redenbach, Linda Sorenson, Maya Sutton, Jerry Tereszkiewicz and Milton Wilson for their invaluable assistance. A special thanks to Dave Bruno for his great generosity in providing a large number of the quotes we've used in this book.

We would also like to thank the following people, who offered continual encouragement, enthusiasm and support throughout our work on this project. These individuals include: Cheryl Cramer, Lisa Cramer, Lynn Cramer, Lynn Dimet, Guadalupe Dominguez, Evonne Fisher, Gerald Gonzalez, Linda Hannan, Joy Jacobson, Paul Jaramillo, Teresa Jaramillo, Lydia Zepeda Jennings, Clarice Johnson, Nancy Knickerbocker, Anna Krezan, David Lang, David Levin, Demetria Martinez, Evelyn Mercur, Terry Ortega, Barbara Ortiz, Carol Park, Rick

Pierson, Aili Pogust, Susan Priest, Lorraine Rariden, Michelle Rathman, Dora and Ernie Sanchez, Jennifer Sanchez, Lila A. Sanchez, Lila J. and Nicolas Sanchez, Nicole Sanchez-Howell, Jeannine Steidl, Sharon Tandy, Frances Varela and Sister Marci Zeiman. Their support enhanced the experience for all of us.

We would also like to acknowledge the remarkable spirit of the individual members of our HCI "family," from their enthusiastic reception of our initial proposal to the strong support and encouragement that kept us on track. We especially would like to thank Theresa Peluso for her assistance regarding some of the more technical aspects of this project, Lisa Bernstein for her astute editing skills and her respect for our vision, and Matthew Diener for his wisdom, guidance and friendship.

A special thank-you to Gus Pomeroy, Susan Schaller, Shelly Nichols and Steve Garcia at Sir Speedy for their generous help in providing copies of the manuscript at various stages of its development. We would also like to acknowledge the owners and staff of the Siam Café, who graciously allowed us to occupy a few booths at a time for dinner meetings that went on forever, as well as Jerry Tereszkiewicz, our "sugar angel," who surprised us with wonderful homemade treats from time to time. And finally, an extra-special thank-you to our furry and feathered friends, Violet, Chelsea and Shadow, for their participation in this project.

Introduction

*I*n the course of a recent dinner conversation, the three of us started comparing our experiences of keeping journals throughout our lives. Starting with the pink vinyl diaries from elementary school (with tiny locks and keys that only barely discouraged curious siblings) and moving through a series of spiral-bound notebooks, we talked about how we might enjoy working with a journal that offered a more structured format. Further, in line with our own personal and spiritual development, we acknowledged the need for a journal that could inspire reflection and encourage documentation, specifically of our gratitude and appreciation for the growth and abundance we had experienced.

We recognized that we probably were not alone in our desire, and decided to create a resource that would help us—and others—to focus thoughts and perceptions in positive directions, to reframe negative events in terms of growth and benefits, and to track and acknowledge insights, accomplishments and the beauty in our lives. We envisioned a book with space for writing, drawing and pasting (collage-style).

We considered various ways to examine our lives in terms of gratitude, which led to the twelve chapters of the journal section of this book. These chapters range from the concrete and tangible (as in "Daily Riches" and "Wonder All Around") to more abstract and ethereal (as in "Magic, Miracles and Synchronicity" and "Dreams and Visions"). There are chapters to help focus on the world around us, the people in our lives, our material possessions, and our own inner

If the only prayer you say in your life is "thank you," that would suffice.
—MEISTER ECKHART

Turn another page. Write something every day. If you don't know how to spell, make it up, draw pictures or doodle. Write something good that happened today. Writing is like talking to someone who is not there.
—MARY CHLOE SCHOOLCRAFT SAUNDERS

resources and self-worth. Some chapters help us reflect on the past with wisdom, perspective and appreciation, while others help us look forward, sharpening our wishes, desires and creative intentions. We also offer chapters to acknowledge the pleasures of both giving and receiving.

While the overall outlook of this journal is emphatically positive and hopeful, we recognize that many readers may come to this resource during a time in their lives that is anything but! Be assured that we have all experienced extended dark periods and events that for years did not make much sense. Even during the writing of this book, each of us confronted tragedies, emotional challenges and major setbacks, experiences that dared us to listen to our own words. We have made every effort to be sensitive to people who may be reading these chapters after or during a life trauma, health crisis or period of particular emotional stress.

We hope, therefore, that this book will help you remember that there is beauty and purpose even in the midst of a bad day or a dark night. While we recognize that challenges are an ongoing part of life, it may help to be mindful of the abundance and magic that are available to comfort you and help you heal—or at least catch your breath. This journal can be a vehicle through which you remember to maintain your connection with the richness and grace in your life, and a way to let them in.

We envision this journal as a place for

validating the good in your life. We also see it as a way to help you reprogram scarcity consciousness, limited thinking and negative expectations, and to shift your thinking in order to emphasize possibilities instead. Perhaps more important, we hope that this journal will help you keep in mind the internal and external power and resources available to you, regardless of anything else that may be going on in your life.

We deliberately did not design this journal in a calendar format so that you don't feel pressure to write every day whether you want to or not, or feel guilty if you fall behind. Instead, we've presented an open-ended format that serves as an invitation to record your thoughts and ideas as the inspiration strikes, at any time throughout the day—or year!

Although we recognize that many people will have no problem starting to write the second they see blank lines on a page, we also realize that others may need a gentle nudge to get them going. We have included in each chapter a set of activities to provide guidance, motivation, inspiration and focus. Some of the activities require specific, structured responses. However, many activities will require no written reflection; some will simply give you something to think about as you go about your day. Allow these activities to inspire you or to help you become more aware of the good that already exists in your life. We invite you to work with your own

Gratitude is free. No chains. No tolls.
—ANDY QUIÑONES

Do your practice patiently and consistently with no thought of the result, and the process will deliver outstanding rewards in due time.
—D. TRINIDAD HUNT

Gratitude makes sense of our past, brings peace for today and creates a vision for tomorrow.
—MELODY BEATTIE

personal style and needs, whether that means doing every activity, choosing those that feel particularly relevant to your current situation, or using the ideas as a jumping-off place for your own free expression. The activities may also be helpful if you want to write but don't know where to start.

Certain activities recommend a specific length of time for writing or the creation of a list of a specific number of items. These suggestions are not meant to limit you in any way; they are there just to get you started. So write. Write as abundantly as you wish.

Don't let the number of questions— either in the text or in the activities themselves—overwhelm you. Feel free to stop at any point to explore, reflect or write; or read through the material and then back up and choose a direction. Skip around as you like. The questions and activities are intended to stimulate and help you focus. Use them in whatever way is most comfortable for you.

If reading the text in any chapter triggers resistance or a negative reaction, we encourage you to read on or to skip to the quotes and activities. Often these sections will be the ones that can serve you best. However, rather than getting stuck, choose a different chapter instead, if necessary. Release any ideas that hold no meaning or relevance for you. Take care of yourself as you intuitively know best.

Use this book if you're having a good day, and especially if you're having a bad one.

One of the surest signs of gratitude is laughter. Humor is a great way to turn gratings into gratitude.
—PETER MCWILLIAMS

It is not possible to feel gratitude and negativity at the same time.
—SHARON WEGSCHEIDER-CRUSE

A journal can be a great release if you're feeling angry, frightened, worried or discouraged. Use what feels useful. Make this journal work for you. Write, draw, doodle, cut or paste. Color outside the lines. Use bigger paper or supplement your journal with a tablet or notebook. There is no one right way.

We hope this book helps you touch the magic in your life, leads to greater expression of the beauty and joy within, and reminds you to tap into the grace and deep wisdom that you already possess.

Gratitude is not only the greatest of virtues, but the parent of all others.
—Cicero

Gratitude is the memory of the heart.
—J. B. Massieu

1

Magic, Miracles and Synchronicity

Even the most ordinary day can be filled with moments of magic and mystery, many of these moments occurring in apparently unspectacular, and often unnoticed, packages. For most of us, the miracles we experience throughout our lives won't involve an audible angelic chorus or great flashes of light. Miraculous moments occur when a baby is born and we count ten toes! It's the feeling we get when we sense that everything in a particular moment has come together in some perfect way. It's the astonishing synergy we some-times sense in a particular group of people, when the magnetic pull between friends or family members brings out their deeper essences. It's the magic we feel after we've had a great conversation, when the excitement of intellectual challenge or stimulation continues to brew, or when the sense of playfulness and spontaneity lingers beyond the actual interaction. These moments occur even if we haven't yet learned to notice them.

Magic appears when we notice events like the changing seasons, a daffodil or tulip pushing through the frozen ground, the crackling autumn leaves, or the unimaginable uniqueness of every snowflake in

1

I left my father's hospital bed, realizing for the first time that he was very, very sick and might not survive this most recent heart attack. As I walked into the vast, open plaza outside the hospital entrance, I sat down at a fountain, the only person in the entire outdoor area. The solitude allowed the stress and grief to catch up with me. In the privacy of the open space, I began to sob. Immediately, there were two hands on my shoulder. A woman had appeared out of nowhere! "I understand," she said. "My mother is in there, too. I just want you to know that you are not alone." I was nearly as surprised as I was comforted. I have never doubted that on that day, I was visited by an angel.

—Jane Bluestein

Living a spiritual life means having God as a background thought. . . . It means living each day in a spirit of gratitude. It means looking for the spark of divine light in everyone you meet regardless of the circumstances. It means to pray without ceasing with the absolute faith that all your prayers will be answered in an abundant universe.

—Philip Oliver-Diaz and Patricia A. O'Gorman

a meadow. It occurs in those moments of quiet reflection, sitting under a tree, bathing in moonlight or looking at sunshine filtered through a piece of stained glass.

There's also magic in abundance, in actually having money seem to drop out of the heavens—a gift, a winning lottery ticket or a crumpled bill we just found in the pocket of a jacket we haven't worn for a while. At the same time, there's magic in the opportunities that come with receiving—a chance to enjoy the windfall, to reconcile feelings of deservingness, to see evidence that we're being well taken care of or to indulge our generosity.

But the magic of abundance is not limited to mere dollars. Our treasure chests also contain gold coins of incredible memories, pearls of wisdom, silver chains of friendship, rubies of health, garnets of talent and diamonds of promise.

We are sometimes surprised by the seemingly perfect timing of some events, often referring to them as lucky, accidental or unbelievable. Just think of those out-of-the-blue phone calls or encounters with someone we were just talking about. Or what about those experiences we call "coincidences," unexpected happenings, favors or surprises, or even déjà vu? Coincidences may seem to occur haphazardly. But what if we shift our frame of reference and think of these moments as synchronistic occurrences? What if we move these events from the realm of the

There are only two ways to live your life. One is as though nothing is a miracle. The other is as though everything is a miracle.
—ALBERT EINSTEIN

Nothing is too good to be true. Nothing is too wonderful to happen.
—CATHERINE PONDER

Sometimes I need to be reminded that there are other options. I thought I was limited to two choices when I learned that the balcony on my condo had been built defectively. The first option was a ten thousand-dollar repair for which I would have to pay. The second option was to replace the balcony—also at my expense—cost as yet unknown. Feeling frustrated with these unsatisfactory options, I told myself there had to be another way that did not involve a cost to me. A few weeks later, at the home-owners' association meeting, we all learned that a solution had been found. The builder who had, years ago, gone bankrupt, was now back in business. As a show of good faith, he agreed to repair all the defective balconies at his own expense. This was a great reminder that more solutions and possibilities can exist than I may immediately see or imagine.

—Janet

Every person, all the events of your life are there because you have drawn them there.

—Richard Bach

random to a context that operates with greater deliberateness—with a deeper purpose and meaning in the grander scheme of our lives and the general flow of the universe?

Magical moments can include those instances in which we narrowly avoid life's little disasters: the apparent intervention that prevents fender benders and wrong turns, helps us think twice before we blurt out something hurtful or insensitive, or triggers our intuition about impending or potential danger we might otherwise not notice. They might include the guidance that allows us to recall an obscure fact we need to pass an exam, to reach the exact person we need to contact to complete certain arrangements, to solve a particular problem or even to find a parking place in an impossibly full lot. These moments give us the feeling that someone is watching over us, helping us navigate life's little twists and turns.

Moments of synchronicity come to us as we catch a certain lyric or a phrase in a book—or perhaps a passing bumper sticker—and are struck by a flash of insight or wisdom. We see just the right item we need in a place we never expected to find it. We get a gut feeling or sense a message from someplace within us—not our minds, but a deep, wise place of knowing—and we suddenly have an answer to a life-changing question.

We not only attract this synchronous

When you get to a fork in the road, take it.
—YOGI BERRA

When God wants a thing done, the speed with which it achieves completion and success almost takes your breath away.
—WAYNE MULLER

My friends from out of town had just called to say they were coming to visit me. I was looking forward to seeing them, but at the same time, I was stressed about how I would handle the visit financially. I was going through an extremely tight financial time and there was a week to go before I would be paid. To this day, I don't know what compelled me to go through that box of books I had sitting in my old car, which hadn't run for more than a year. So imagine my astonishment when I opened one book and found eighty dollars stashed there. This was exactly enough to go out with my friends and be able to enjoy our time together without the worry of money.

—SUZANNE

We have what we seek. It is there all the time, and if we give it time it will make itself known to us.

—THOMAS MERTON

energy, but we also help create it! Every day offers numerous opportunities for us to initiate whimsical magic, abundant miracles and exquisite timing. This can happen when we walk down the street humming or when we use a fairy-godmother voice to whisper something reassuring to a young child. It can happen when we enjoy an ice cream cone with an isolated neighbor or reach out anonymously with a kind act. We may hear others wonder, *Why are you doing that?* Perhaps they are also wondering why they aren't doing the same. Our joy and magic will continue to ripple out as inspiration, and will deepen and strengthen the vibration of kindness, caring and love.

We can recognize that there are wonderful little things that go right in our lives. Remembering and recording what could otherwise be overlooked as insignificant helps us reinforce the numerous small, joyous wonders we experience. Use the journal pages in this chapter to create or increase your awareness. Keep track of the magic, miracles and synchronicity that occur in the course of your day. Notice events that appear to be coincidental. Describe surprise meetings and unexpected gifts. Acknowledge the voice of your own intuition. This process of recording will focus your attention on the sweet moments in your life. It will also clear the negative dust off your psychic magnets, creating a stronger attraction for even more magic in your life.

Coincidence is God's way of performing a miracle anonymously.
—AUTHOR UNKNOWN

I don't feel that I have to worry about what's going to happen tomorrow, because I know that the next step just keeps on appearing on my pathway. I often don't know exactly what it will be. But, looking back, I can see that it has always been the right thing.
—MERLIN STONE

I was working at a hospice center when a Native American man came in with the most unusual and beautiful jewelry. I couldn't resist a pair of malachite and silver earrings, even though I was saving money to go back to college. I later learned that one of his children had recently died in our hospice. The next week when I was at the gym, I forgot those earrings, which had quickly become my favorites. When I called the gym, I was told that the earrings had been found and would be kept in a safe, but the next day, the earrings were gone. I knew that I would have to return to school without my earrings, certain that they had been lost forever. My mom asked me if I really wanted to find them. When I said yes, she said I would truly have to believe they would be returned. I said that I did, but in a rather pitiful voice. She asked me to keep saying "I believe it" until I finally sounded like I really meant it! Two weeks later I received a care package from my mom, and among the items was an envelope that said "Do You Believe?" When I opened it, there were the earrings! They had shown up at the gym after all!

—NICOLE

The thing that is important is the thing that is not seen.
—ANTOINE DE SAINT-EXUPÉRY

Tune in to your very own harmonious pattern of life's treasures and the flow that brings you to your own center. This book is designed to help bring you to that place, a place in which you become a source of magic, miracles and synchronicity—both for yourself and for others.

In order to be a realist, you must believe in miracles.

—DAVID BEN-GURION

ACTIVITIES

- Complete the following sentence with as many examples as you can think of: "I am truly grateful for the magic, miracles and synchronicity in my life, including _____." Add to this list whenever you wish.

- Write the word "intuition." Set a timer for five minutes and without stopping to think or question your thoughts, write down any ideas that come to mind with regard to this topic.

- Write about what you would do if you knew you absolutely could not fail.

- Start keeping track of special unexpected gifts, or surprise encounters or phone calls that come into your life. Note any intuitive messages or gut feelings you experience. Identify events that give you chills or goose bumps.

- Start paying attention to evidence of intuitiveness. Listen to yourself and others for key phrases such as "I knew this was going to happen" or "I had a feeling about this." Look for examples of people acknowledging or acting on their intuition and write them down.

- Identify movies you have seen that had magic, miracles or synchronicity for you. Watch them again. See how the magic affects or inspires you this time.

- Ask friends and relatives to describe a magical or miraculous moment in their lives. Record the parts of their stories that touch you.

- Ponder the magic and mystery in a child's life. Write about the magic you experienced as a child or the magic you wished you had experienced.

- Encourage your children to keep a journal for reflection in the future. Have them record their dreams.

- Describe an example of something that seemed like a coincidence or accident. Reflect on the synchronistic sequence of events, the perfect timing and how the occurrence may have served your life.

- Write your own mealtime grace, bedtime prayer or gratitude prayer. If possible, type it and illustrate it. Laminate or frame it and keep it handy to use often.

- In what ways are you able to receive graciously—including being able to receive compliments, gifts, kindness, money or generosity from others? Which are easier for you to receive? Which are more difficult? If receiving anything has been difficult for you, you may want to explore your resistance in your journal, or you may prefer to name one new thing you can do to allow yourself to receive with greater ease or less discomfort. Add to this list whenever possible.

The word "intuition" comes from the same root as the word "contemplate." It means sensing without the use of rational processes. In one way or another, you've been following your intuition since you were born. You may have become disconnected from it; you may have ignored it, betrayed it or invalidated it, but there is a footpath in your mind that has led you there again and again.

—DAWNA MARKOVA

*Happiness sneaks in
through a door you
didn't know you left
open.*
—JOHN BARRYMORE

*Miracles are not
contrary to nature, but
only contrary to what
we know about nature.*

—ST. AUGUSTINE OF HIPPO

*The beauty of intuition
includes whispers of
wisdom, guidance and
inspiration. Intuitive
revelations often ride
the express train to the
truth, arriving at the
conclusion ahead of
the reasoning process
that will eventually lead
to the same conclusion.*
—SAGE BENNET

It's easy to assume that life-changing spiritual experiences must be spectacular, that they must deal with great problems. But spiritual growth involves every-day moments of living. Any simple event or combination of events can be the occasion for spiritual enlightenment and transformation.

—"God Moments"
introduction, *Unity Magazine*

*The universe within us
is rich and powerful,
and intuitively we know
this; we already know
we have everything we
need, so there really is
no need to be attached
to anything.*
—SHAKTI GAWAIN

*This is the task of the
mystic: to live in
gratitude and let
gratitude radiate
wherever you are.*

—Caroline Myss

Spiritual truth is not something elaborate and esoteric, it is in fact profound common sense.

—SOGYAL RINPOCHE

*Each friend represents
a world in us, a world
possibly not born until
they arrive, and it is
only by this meeting
that a new world is
born.*

—Anaïs Nin

All the family
In harmony
Laughing and laughing . . .
This is the original
Music of Nature.

—JAPANESE FOLK ZEN SAYING

*If you surrendered to
the air, you could ride it.*

—Toni Morrison

We can live in a world of reality only if we have a taste for mystery.
—M. Scott Peck

God writes in exceedingly crooked lines.

—César Chávez

What used to be the hunch or the occasional inspiration gradually becomes a working part of the mind.

—ALCOHOLICS ANONYMOUS

Nothing real can be threatened. Nothing unreal exists.

—A COURSE IN MIRACLES

2

Wonder All Around

*H*ave you ever received a postcard from a place so beautiful that you stopped to imagine what living in a place like that must be like? Have you ever suspected that doing laundry or paying bills would somehow be a lot less tedious in Tahiti, Paris or the Himalayas?

There is beauty all around us, no matter where we live. But even people living in the most beautiful surroundings can become oblivious to the richness in their environment when the details of daily life take over. Seeing the wonder all around us requires a certain deliberateness and mindfulness. If you already live in a place you consider to be beautiful, or if you have at some point relocated to a particular place *because* of its beauty, then this awareness may come easily to you. However, you may live in a place that requires that you look a little harder to find—or notice—the beauty around you.

You may also need to broaden your definitions of beauty and wonder. Truly fortunate are those who can find resplendence in any environment, whether glimpsing a road through a rural cornfield, watching storm clouds blanket a crowded city, or seeing a sunset embroider a snow-covered mountain. But it's not necessary to leave home or travel

I have a friend who travels a lot. I always anticipate special postcards from her. They not only show where she is, but give me a chance to experience the beauty and magic of some far-off place with her.

—LYNN COLLINS

Being from the suburb of a big city, the wild places have long enticed me to explore their awe-inspiring secrets. One day on a hike in Glacier Park, a granddaddy of a bighorn sheep wheeled to a halt in front of me and licked my hand rather than pitching me off a mountain ledge. Another time, an inquisitive, bright-eyed red fox peeked at us all during dinner at our Isle Royale campsite. Friends and I once quietly cross-country skied past a huge moose contentedly drinking from a lake in the Tetons. One golden autumn morning in the Canadian Rockies, we awoke to a male elk rearing back his head and bugling into the frosty air, and a few hours later, encountered a silver-tipped grizzly rooting through newly fallen snow for dinner roots. I remain blessed by these moments of wild serendipity and the sheer magnificence of the natural wonders on this planet, and I'm grateful for having stepped off the beaten path long enough to have experienced them.

—LINDA SORENSON

Seeing is different from being told.

—KENYAN PROVERB

to exotic lands to experience beauty. Sometimes, it's just a matter of seeing. Remember, somewhere out there, a visitor may be sending someone a picture post-card of your hometown.

Go to a window or step outside. Look around. Notice the lines and curves, the tex-tures, shadows and colors in the buildings on your block. Witness the miracle of a flower growing through a crack in the side-walk or in a vacant lot. Allow a sunset to take your breath away. Recognize the adventure of the changing seasons in the gentle beauty of a fallen leaf. Lie down on your roof or lawn and float along with the clouds.

Observe. Receive. Connect.

Listen to the sacred symphony of waves breaking on the beach. Chase a rainbow or a shooting star. Notice how many shades of green can be produced by nature in a gar-den or park. Taste the temperature of a warm summer breeze. Wrap yourself in the colors of a stormy afternoon. Go for a walk in a different part of town. Let the sparkle of sunlight on a stream hypnotize you.

Open your eyes. Take in the beauty of where you are right now. Even if you've never before appreciated the local environ-mental ambience, it's all there, all around you—beauty and wonder in immeasurable supply. And it's all for you!

Enjoy!

Joy is what happens when we allow ourselves to recognize how good things are. . . . Joy is what happens when we see that God's plan is perfect and we're already starring in a perfect show.
—MARIANNE WILLIAMSON

Whether we look, or whether we listen, we hear life murmur, or see it glisten.
—JAMES RUSSELL LOWELL

The other night, my phone rang. When I answered, I was greeted with a friend's excited voice: "Go look out your front window," she said, and then hung up. Curious, I put the receiver back and walked to the front of my house. There behind the mountains I could see a powerful glow preceding what, in the next minute or two, would be an enormous, beautiful full moon. Suddenly, I could no longer remember what had been bothering me minutes before the call. All the troubles of the day disappeared as I gazed at the sky. This was the most precious gift I'd received in a long time.

—DONNA

I saw a distant river by moonlight, making no noise, yet flowing, as by day, still to the sea, like melted silver reflecting the moonlight. . . .There is a certain glory attends on a water by night. By it the heavens are related to the earth, undistinguishable from a sky beneath you.

—HENRY DAVID THOREAU

The morning glory which blooms an hour differs not at heart from the giant pine which lives for a thousand years.

—ALAN WATTS

ACTIVITIES

- Complete the following sentence with as many examples as you can think of: "I am truly grateful for the gift of beauty in my environment as it is reflected in _____." Add to this list whenever you wish.

- Write the word "beauty." Set a timer for five minutes and without stopping to think or question your thoughts, write down any ideas that come to mind with regard to this topic.

- Go to a local drugstore or souvenir shop. Purchase a few postcards of the place where you live. Send a postcard of your hometown to a friend. Send another to yourself.

- Take a day off—or a few hours—to visit attractions around your town or state. See your hometown as a visitor or tourist might see it.

- Take a walk and notice five new things you've never noticed before.

- Take a walk with a camera. Whether or not you actually take any pictures, look through the lens to see your world differently or notice different things. (Try this with a telescope or binoculars, too! Even a rolled-up piece of paper creates a new perspective.)

- Sit in a comfortable room and describe the different colors and textures you see.

- Find a comfortable place outside to sit for at least five to ten minutes. Close your eyes and notice how many different sounds you can hear. (For example, listen for sounds of different birds, insects and animals, traffic sounds, water sprinklers or rain, wind, human voices, rustling leaves or other sounds in nature.)

- Set your alarm to awaken you before daybreak if you don't ordinarily arise at this time of day. Find a space where you can enjoy and welcome the dawn.

- Wander through a farmers' market or a flower market. Experience the sensory delights of colors, textures, smells, designs, shapes, shadows and sounds.

- On a clear evening, drive far enough away from city lights to watch the stars. Take a lounge chair or a blanket and maybe a friend. Explore the sky. Find a constellation or two. Look for shooting stars.

My hut's roof is
The blue heavens;
Floor, the earth;
Lamps, the sun and moon;
Hand-broom, the wind.

—JAPANESE FOLK ZEN SAYING

The new voyage of discovery consists not in seeking new landscapes but in having new eyes.

—MARCEL PROUST

Every part of this earth is sacred to my people. Every shining pine needle, every sandy shore, every mist in the dark woods, every clearing, and every humming insect is wholly in the memory and experience of my people.

—CHIEF SEALTH (SEATTLE)

Where do people from
Hawaii go on their
honeymoon?
—JIM LIVOLSI

*It's always
your next move.*
—NAPOLEON HILL

Do what intrigues you,
explore what interests
you; think mystery,
not mastery.

—Julia Cameron

We do not remember days, we remember moments.

—Cesare Pavese

*Never before have I
lived through a storm
like the one this
night. . . . The sea has
a look of indescribable
grandeur, especially
when the sun falls on
it. One feels as if one
is dissolved and
merged into Nature.
Even more than usual,
one feels the insignifi-
cance of the individual,
and it makes one
happy.*

—ALBERT EINSTEIN

Seeing the sacred in ourselves and in all living things is the solution.

—GLORIA STEINEM

Steep thyself in a bowl of summertime.

—VIRGIL

*How many of you
have walked your own
property, considering it
a sacred space, and let
Earth know how much
you treasure it?*

—BARBARA MARCINIAK

You only live once—but
if you work it right,
once is enough.

—JOE E. LEWIS

Your world is abundant
with all that you con-
sider to be good, and
you have easy access
to that abundance.
—JERRY AND ESTHER HICKS

*The critical action
of considering the
miraculous includes
looking for and
treasuring the
manifestations of
God's miraculous
work in the concrete
circumstances of life.*

—GLENNA SALSBURY

Nature is always talking about growth. It's always talking about change, ways of movement, ways things will develop and deal with obstacles, showing how water will flow around a boulder rather than smack into it all the time. We can see in nature all the answers to everything we need to know.

—MERLIN STONE

3

Dreams and Visions

Somewhere between the details of day-to-day living, amid the clutter of inescapable mental checklists, our minds are creating, receiving, collecting. Even while we sleep, work, interact with one another, play, relax or go about our lives, there are moments of simply knowing and imagining. Inspiration and insight may come at any time. Our inner processes happen continually and automatically, regardless of the amount of distraction we are experiencing. Sometimes we are fortunate enough to notice.

This chapter will help you pay attention to your hunches, your intuition, or any guidance that may appear to you through visions or dreams. Often these insights will present themselves in the most subtle packages, and they may be easy to overlook or dismiss. Use the journal pages in this chapter to jot down the thoughts you notice, in whatever form they appear to you. Recording these "messages" helps you stay tuned in—awake and receptive—even when you don't exactly understand what the messages mean.

For example, pay attention to the colors, conversations, images, feelings or sensations you encounter in a dream or a fantasy. By

I have this recurring dream in which I'm wandering through a house I know well. It's always a different house, but I have this sense that I live there. In each case, I discover, with surprise and some confusion, a door or a hallway I had never noticed before. In each dream, this discovery leads to a room, often a maze of rooms or an entire wing I never knew existed. For a long time I just assumed the dreams reflected a shortage of closet space in my life. Looking back, though, I always seem to experience this dream during periods of significant change, growth or personal discovery.

—MONA

If one door closes, just know there are bigger and better doors trying to open.

—CATHERINE PONDER

Your dreams are not meant to put you to sleep, but to alert and arouse you to your immense possibilities.

—DAVID PHILLIPS

remembering and recording these details, you acknowledge the information and reinforce your accountability to your own consciousness. Regardless of your interpretation, regardless of any action you take, you're present and aware. You're listening.

If a moment of silence or meditation triggers something significant, profound or insightful, here is a place to capture its essence. Do you notice a recurring theme? Where have your fantasies taken you lately? Be aware of any images in which you find yourself in unlikely situations, activities or locations.

Pay attention to the little voice in the back of your mind or those feelings in your gut. What are they saying? Where are they leading you? For example, if you experience a persistent urge to add "Quit this dead-end job" somewhere between "Pick up the dry cleaning" and "Call Mom" on your daily to-do lists, you may want to honor this insight on the pages that follow. Make a note of that weird flash that came to you right before you fell asleep last night. What about the idea that occurred to you in the middle of the movie you were watching last week? More than one great song, book, design, invention, change or idea started as a jumble of words scrawled on a nightstand scratch pad in the deepest dark of night.

Write it down. Draw your dream.

Observe where, when and under what circumstances you feel the most clear or receptive. When do ideas come to you?

Imagination is the eye of the soul.
—Joseph Joubert

The dreamers are the saviours of the world.
—James Allen

Dreams are the soul's pantry. Keep it well stocked, and your soul will never hunger.
—Shirley Feeney
(of TV's *Laverne and Shirley*)

I've never been one for quiet introspection on mountaintops. I get too distracted by the sights, sounds and smells up there, not to mention wind, bugs and imperfect temperatures. I admire people who can sit still long enough to clear their minds, and for a long time believed that there was something wrong with me because I never felt right on that path. I do know that doing certain things with my hands, repetitive things like knitting or stitching or spinning, grounds me—energetically and spiritually—like nothing else can. The fiber is my rosary, the motion my meditation. There is no question in my mind that this is a legitimate way to connect with God.

—JANINE

It may be more effective for some people to walk when they meditate, and it does not mean they are spiritually remedial if they cannot sit still for an hour.

—DAWNA MARKOVA

In each of us are heroes; speak to them, and they will come forth.

—ANONYMOUS

How do you fulfill that critical need for a quiet moment to pause and reflect? Do you make time to tune in to the guidance available to you? How do you remind yourself to pay attention, to listen and receive?

Also, think about what you may be doing to *block* inspiration, to not notice or remember what your mind creates. How do you react to the voice of inspiration? Notice if there is another voice dismissing what you've heard. What is it saying? Write it down.

Record an impulse, describe a vision, invite an answer, scribble a daydream, imagine a possibility, ask "What if?" or render the texture of a dream. Do not hold back—or at least notice when you do! Your mind is a treasure chest, bottomless, limitless.

Peek inside.

And write down what you find.

Destiny is done one day at a time.
—D. TRINIDAD HUNT

Try asking yourself from time to time, "Am I awake now?"
—JON KABAT-ZINN

I've always been able to remember my dreams, often in vivid detail. I consider myself fortunate in this. But I've often found that my most inspired "dreams" neither needed nor waited for me to fall asleep. In the shower, while I'm driving or chopping vegetables, often as I turn out the light just before I fall asleep, I'll get a picture in my mind, a word, an idea, an answer to a question. When I stop and listen, the information always comes.

—Monika

I had a counselor who used to remind me that the messages were always coming through, even though I felt frustrated that I wasn't hearing them. She reminded me that the guidance was like the radio towers on the mountain, which are continually emitting clear signals whether the radio is on or not, or whether people are tuned in to the actual station or just picking up static.

—Zoe

If I do not go within, I go without.

—Neale Donald Walsch

Inner guidance is always there inside us, and it is always correct, wise and loving. We may lose touch with it, or misinterpret it at times. We may try to push too hard and get ahead of ourselves. But our inner teacher never abandons us. We are never alone.

—Shakti Gawain

ACTIVITIES

- Complete the following sentence with as many examples as you can think of: "I am truly grateful for the gift of imagination as it is reflected in _____." Add to this list whenever you wish.

- Write the word "inspiration." Set a timer for five minutes and without stopping to think or question your thoughts, write down any ideas that come to mind with regard to this topic.

- Write the following sentence on a piece of paper: "I clearly remember my dreams." Keep the paper next to your bed and remember to read this sentence (out loud if you can) right before you turn out the light. When you awaken, lie in bed quietly with your eyes closed, without talking or interacting with anyone else, if possible. (If you can, set your alarm a few minutes early.) Reflect on any dream images or sequences that came to you during the night, recalling as much detail as possible.

- Write down your dreams. You can use individual words or simple phrases, or more elaborate sentences with as many details as you recall. Capture as much of the feeling and essence of the dream as you can. Do not worry about interpretation. Focus on description. Note: If you tend not to remember your dreams, record images from a daydream, a fantasy, a meditation, an inspiration, or however thoughts and images come to you.

- Is there a dream or image that you used to have, either as a recurring phenomenon or a vision so strong you've never forgotten it? Write down as much as you remember.

- If you have a question or problem currently challenging you, write it down before you go to bed. Use as much detail as possible to ask for specific information as well as general guidance. Note the kind of images and information that come to you in your dreams and throughout the following day or days.

- After you've been recording your dreams for a while (or if you've been keeping a dream journal for some time), go back and read over your dreams. See if you can find any trends, patterns or reflections of things occurring in your life at that time.

- Describe a dream, daydream, vision, meditation or reflection that helped you make a decision or gave you an answer.

- Identify three to five things you do that help you feel grounded, centered, focused and calm. Make time for one of them (for at least ten minutes or more) in the next few days. Add more centering or calming activities to this list whenever possible.

- Draw your dream, make a collage representing images in a dream, or collect pictures or phrases from magazines that reflect your fantasies and visions.

- Describe a déjà vu experience you've had, or some experience in which you felt some form of precognition or unexplained familiarity with a particular person, place or situation.

- Keep a notepad or some scratch paper next to your bed, in your briefcase or purse, in your car and around your office and home. As ideas and impressions come to you, jot them down (or use a tape recorder).

- Vision yourself: Picture yourself in a job, relationship, vacation retreat, hobby or fun activity, car or situation you desire. Notice as many details as you possibly can, accounting for all your senses, if possible. (In other words, how do you look? How do you feel? What colors, furniture, plants, textures, people or environmental features surround you? Notice smells, how the air feels, specifically what you are doing.) Write, draw or make a collage of this image and add to it as you wish.

*The unexamined life
is not worth living.*
—Socrates

*What we consciously
fail to see is frequently
perceived by our
unconscious, which
can pass the infor-
mation on through
dreams. . . . Dream
symbols are the essen-
tial message-carriers
from the instinctive to
the rational parts of
the human mind.*

—CARL JUNG

*The problem isn't
having it all but
receiving it all, giving
ourselves permission
to have a full and
passionate life. . . .
The biggest limit to our
having is our small
reach, our shy embrace.*

—Marianne Williamson

*The poverty-conscious
fear that keeps us from
slowing down is perhaps
the most insidious bar-
rier of all to prosperity.
Most major achievers in
this world have reported
that they made some
powerful breakthroughs
after taking time out for
contemplation and
reassessment.*
—JERRY GILLIES

*Imagination is more
important than
knowledge.*

—ALBERT EINSTEIN

Imagination is the highest kite one can fly.

—LAUREN BACALL

*We are so busy focusing
on action that we have
forgotten the art of
contemplation.*
—PHILIP OLIVER-DIAZ AND
    PATRICIA A. O'GORMAN

Fear is static that prevents me from hearing my intuition.

—HUGH PRATHER

These voices have information for you— all of it useful. Some you can use by following; others you can use by doing precisely the opposite. It's a matter of knowing whether or not a given voice is on your side.

—Peter McWilliams

Nowhere in the spiritual literature, as far as I know, is there one reported incident of a person regretting following Divine guidance.

—CAROLINE MYSS

The power of our minds to dream, to imagine and to create visions is one of our greatest and [most] important gifts. For out of the realm of the imagined can come the ideas we can use to create everything from a work of art, to a life-changing discovery.

—Morgan Simone Daleo

Make your mind
Flexible as water:
Now square,
Now round—up to
The shape of the bowl.
—JAPANESE FOLK ZEN SAYING

We may feel—and look—erratic. This erraticism is a normal part of getting unstuck, pulling free from the muck that has blocked us. . . . At first flush, going sane feels just like going crazy.
—JULIA CAMERON

Practice creative listening. Get quiet so that insights can come through your mind.

—NORMAN VINCENT PEALE

A mind too active is no mind at all.

—THEODORE ROETHKE

4

Daily Riches

*L*ook at the daily riches that abound in our everyday lives. How many of these comforts do we take for granted? Basic conveniences like refrigerators, bathrooms, hot water, telephones, mailboxes—and mail service, too—can take on a whole new perspective after even a brief visit to a location in which these amenities do not exist. Most of us have worked hard for the abundance we enjoy. For many of us, our lives include a number of comforts we may no longer even notice. The riches that surround us can range from having a comfortable roof over our heads or clean, running water to beautiful artwork, stocked bookshelves and state-of-the-art electronics.

Why not take a moment to stop and appreciate your surroundings and the conveniences available to you? Are you able to heat up a quick meal because of your microwave or toaster oven? Does having a VCR allow you to watch a favorite program or movie at your leisure? Have you noticed how handy the garage door opener is on a rainy night? Even appliances we say we hate to use come in really handy when it's time to vacuum our carpets, mow our lawns or wash our clothes.

I returned home after five days of camping in spectacular mountains where we hiked and fished and lay around under brilliant starry skies, eating S'mores. Although I had had a fantastic time, it had never felt so good to take a long, relaxing shower and wash my hair in warm water, eat at our kitchen table, wash dishes in hot, soapy water, and sleep deeply in my comfortable bed!

—TERESA

I was introducing a unit on electricity to a group of fourth-graders, asking them to imagine how life might have been different for kids their age a hundred years or so ago. One student noted that there would have been no TV. "That's right," I confirmed. Another student looked at me, puzzled —the idea was almost too much for her. "What did they watch?" she asked!

—CARLA

Joy is an infinite commodity
and is its own reason for being.

—DONALD CURTIS

The technology that has become available in the past few years has opened a world of services and conveniences. For example, have you used a computer, fax machine, cell phone, calculator, answering machine or copier in the past few days? Consider how much these tools enhance our lives, save us time and improve our ability to communicate with one another. Look at how the technology of the Internet has made it easier for many of us to stay in touch with faraway family or friends, gather information about practically anything, or conduct financial transactions without leaving our desks.

Take in the beauty that surrounds you in your home. Are your plants thriving and continuing to share their bright, healthy colors with you? When you look at a particular wall hanging or art piece, does it bring you pleasure, or take you back to an enjoyable time? You may have a variety of tapes and CDs, or a radio to enjoy while relaxing on your comfortable furniture, reading a selection of magazines and books available to you. Or perhaps your home is more beautiful because of a project you completed using your shop equipment, sewing machine or gardening tools. If you've ever enjoyed the warmth of a crackling fire, the coziness of a down comforter or the cool relief of a good air conditioner, you know the simple pleasures these comforts can provide.

Do you have a place where you can

I'd rather have roses on my table than diamonds on my neck.
—EMMA GOLDMAN

Contentment is natural wealth.
—SOCRATES

One bright November day, a small, color-splashed chunk of concrete tumbled into my hands. It still conjures up strong memories as I recall the source of that concrete—the Berlin Wall—once a symbol of hate and separation, but changed forever in one shining moment. My friend Vigdis and I witnessed people stride into freedom as others pummeled the wall with humble hammers and chisels—fueled by the blood and tears of all those who went before. A young German banged furiously at the graffiti-covered wall near me, launching a bright, palm-sized piece of wall into my hands. However, the most profound moment came later as we sipped coffee in a café and spotted an elderly gentleman who had just crossed into freedom, nearly floating by the window amidst the throngs. His eyes tilted upward in total awe, sheer amazement spilling over at the spectacle of freedom before him. He was lit from within, and the joy he radiated was so palpable that it nearly took my breath away. How could anyone raised in freedom ever comprehend the deep sense of elation and gratitude in that beautiful face? It's a vision I treasure every time my eye rests on my personal piece of a miracle.

—LINDA SORENSON

A heart at rest sees a feast in everything.

—HINDU PROVERB

appreciate and enjoy the beauty of the environment—perhaps a rooftop patio, a front porch or a nearby park bench? When you run out of milk, you probably don't even think twice about whether it will be available before you go to the store to pick up some more, perhaps at odd hours. Look at the number of places around to shop, see a movie, grab a bite to eat, make copies, get gas, rent a video or use the services of a bank—in many cases, at any time of the day or night.

What other daily riches do you enjoy? Think about the abundance of choices in our lives that continue to expand every day. Never before have we had as many choices available to us, whether we're selecting clothing, pet toys, office supplies, coffee, bottled water, running shoes, the color of our cars or our long-distance telephone carrier. Many of us have access to merchandise and supplies from every corner of the globe right at our fingertips. We can now shop for many of the goods we desire through a nearly unlimited variety of catalogs, over the Internet or from television.

How fortunate we are to have the abundance of choices and variety of selection we now have in almost every facet of our personal and professional lives. (Sometimes the sheer number of choices we have can be a bit overwhelming!) Consider and enjoy the many options you already have for making your life more convenient, beautiful, comfortable and satisfying. Look

Reflect upon your present blessings, of which every man has many; not on your past misfortune, of which all men have some.
—CHARLES DICKENS

After seventeen hours of labor and finally the delivery of my wonderful son, I took the most memorable shower of my life. It was the longest and most relaxing shower one could ever imagine. Standing there, I could feel the hours of sweat and stress melt away. I felt so thin and light as I stood there without that ten pounds that my son weighed—it felt more like twenty-five pounds were gone!

—LORRAINE

Learn to dance with life. It will dip you and spin you,
but when you learn to handle it gracefully,
it turns into something beautiful.

—MARY CHLOE SCHOOLCRAFT SAUNDERS

around at the little things you may take for granted and try to imagine what your life would be like without them. Start to notice the daily riches that are evidence of the prosperity in your everyday life, and acknowledge that these things represent only the tip of the iceberg in the sea of abundance that is possible—and already exists—in your life.

Refuse nothing that comes to you. Pursue nothing that leaves you.
—ZEN SAYING

ACTIVITIES

- Complete the following sentence with as many examples as you can think of: "I am truly grateful for the daily riches in my life, including _____." Add to this list whenever you wish.

- Write the word "abundance." Set a timer for five minutes and without stopping to think or question your thoughts, write down any ideas that come to mind with regard to this topic.

- Before you go to bed, make a list of at least ten daily riches that surround you. Add to this list whenever you wish.

- Look at the items you have in your living space at home. Notice the textures, designs, color and style of your furniture, wall hangings, window coverings and any other items that please you. Write down what you enjoy most about the touch or sight of these possessions.

- Review pictures, knickknacks, photos, trophies, books and any other items you brought back with you from a trip or event where you had a wonderful time. Use these as daily opportunities to remind yourself of the rich memories you carry with you every day.

- Go into your closet and notice your favorite clothes. Which ones make you feel comfortable, confident, sensual?

- Go a whole day noticing the appliances and other conveniences you use, appreciating them and using them consciously.

- Make a list of ten great things about your car. You can also do this activity focusing on ten great things about your home, your computer, your hobby equipment or anything else that has meaning for you.

- Sit in a room in your house or apartment. Make a list of everything in that room, on the walls, in your drawers. Be specific and detailed. Notice what you have in your life! (Alternate activities: List everything on one shelf in your pantry, in the "junk drawer," in your jewelry box, on your workbench or in a corner of your garage. Another way to develop an appreciation of the sheer quantity of daily riches in your life is to make an inventory of everything you own for insurance purposes.)

- Make a list of conveniences, merchandise or services available to you today that did not exist when you were growing up (or even ten or fifteen years ago).

Your task is not to worry over what has been or what will be, but to focus on the joy and happiness that exist right now. All power takes place in the present moment.

—SINDA JORDAN

When we allow our expectations to dissolve, we become more open to the fullness of the moment, open to appreciate the richness of our lives. And as we learn to give thanks for all life, we become more fully alive.

—WAYNE MULLER

*Don't delay your own
prosperity by being
resentful or jealous that
someone else has more
than you. . . . Each
person is under the
law of his or her own
consciousness. Just
take care of your own
thoughts. Bless
another's good fortune,
and know there is
plenty for all.*
—LOUISE L. HAY

*A comfortable house
is a great source of
happiness. It ranks
immediately after health
and a good conscience.*

—Sydney Smith

*Live in each season as
it passes; breathe the
air; drink the drink,
taste the fruit, and
resign yourself to the
influence of each. . . .
Be blown on by all the
winds. Open all your
pores and bathe in all
the tides of nature,
in all her streams and
oceans, at all seasons.*

—HENRY DAVID THOREAU

This is an example we should follow—to bless what we have, know it flows from a limitless Source, and that we merely use and distribute it. There is always more. The limitless resources of Spirit are at our command.

—ERNEST HOLMES

To attain knowledge,
add things every day.
To attain wisdom,
remove things every day.
—*TAO TE CHING*

*Until you make peace
with who you are,
you'll never be content
with what you have.*

—Doris Mortman

Often it is difficult to know what you do want until you get rid of what you do not want.

—CATHERINE PONDER

You can't have everything. Where would you put it?

—Steven Wright

I don't want to be saved. I want to be spent.

—FRITZ PERLS

*All things are possible
to him who believes.*
—MARK 9:22

*We need to be asking
what it is that enlivens,
empowers, excites us,
turns us on, makes us
genuinely feel satisfied
and fulfilled. That's
what actually heals us,
and heals the world.*

—SHAKTI GAWAIN

5

Angels in Disguise

*I*f we could hear the bells that ring every time an Angel touches our lives, we would be enchanted by the symphony that continually surrounds and engulfs us. There is not one hour of our day that legions of Angels do not contribute to our comfort, peace, beauty and synchronicity. Angels may be seen or unseen, and are active in our lives whether we're aware of their presence or not. Often our Angels show up in physical form, as people we encounter on a day-to-day basis, contributing to the quality of our lives.

These are individuals whose unselfish acts are so conspicuous that we can't help but recognize them for what they are: Angels! Blatant Angels! Think of the teachers who make such a difference in our children's lives, the caregivers who nurture the elderly, or firefighters and emergency workers who routinely risk their lives in the service of others. Or consider the physical, mental and spiritual well-being made available through the caring of nurses, doctors, hospice workers, counselors and therapists, midwives, healers, and religious and spiritual leaders. And how about those Angels who take us under their wings and love us—the aunties and uncles, the grandmas and

I peeked out my country window just after dawn one summer morning. To my surprise and delight, a beautiful Siamese cat had found her way to my flower garden. I offered her milk. She accepted, on her own terms, of course, and then disappeared. Day after day, this scenario repeated until one day she stayed. That was over seventeen years ago. Petting her graceful but aging body, I reflect on how much Kiki has enriched my life. Blessings indeed come in all sizes, shapes and species.

—Marcia Kons

When we realize that we are all part of each other,
it is easy to become caregivers.

—Sylvia Boorstein

grandpas who always seem to be there when we need them?

Then there are the everyday Angels, the Angels of service who bring a certain ease, flow and beauty to our lives. How much more effortless are our lives because of the presence of people who cut our hair, deliver our mail, design our clothes and jewelry, bag our groceries, pick up our trash, sew our quilts, and make our bread, cheese, wine and chocolate? Has anyone helped you lately by cleaning your home, walking your dog, mowing your lawn, fixing your car, repairing your appliances, typing your reports, watching your children or helping you find a solution to a problem that's been driving you crazy? These are all Angels in disguise.

Some are hidden Angels, anonymous and silent, people behind the scenes. They are the farmworkers in the fields, the factory workers, the cooks and waitresses who get up before dawn to make our coffee and biscuits. Anonymous Angels include the workers who keep our parks green and clean, the utility workers who fix a power line in the middle of a blizzard, the people who set up carnivals and concerts, and pro-grammers who strive to make computers more user-friendly.

There are special helper Angels who make our lives simpler, smoother and more serene. They're the ones who let us know we're in the wrong line before we've wasted an hour there, the person in an

God has delegated himself to a million deputies.
—RALPH WALDO EMERSON

When eating bamboo sprouts, remember the man who planted them.
—CHINESE PROVERB

My life was falling apart. My husband had recently left me for another woman and was probably taking my oldest daughter with him. There was a restraining order preventing me from going near his place of business, which was just off a main street I often traveled. On the way back from the attorney's office, I realized that I was passing my husband's workplace when I saw the lights on the patrol car behind me come on. We pulled over right in front of my husband's business and as the officer approached my window, I lost it completely. "Having a bad day?" he asked. Sobbing, I nodded and told him what was going on. "Plus, I'm not allowed to be here," I cried. He said he understood. "If anyone says anything, I'll let them know that you're here because of me. I just pulled you over to let you know that your license plates had expired." Instead of a ticket, he wrote up a warning and then, noticing a ticket on my dashboard—a ticket my husband had gotten a week before and had left for me to pay—the officer took enough cash out of his wallet to cover the ticket and handed it to me. This was about the first thing that had gone right all day, and it sure turned me around. I look forward to paying him back, and thanking him for restoring a sense of hope in my life.

—LORETTA

office who knows how to cut through the bureaucracy and red tape to enable us to get our most immediate needs met. They're the resource Angels who know how to find exactly the right telephone number, article, catalog, class, person, tool, software short-cut, clothing accessory or household item.

Some Angels will seem to appear from out of nowhere, to comfort, reassure or guide us just when we need them most. They are responsible for those synchronistic phone calls we receive when we don't even realize we need someone to talk to. They give us a compliment on an insecure day. They make a supposedly innocent comment that has far greater significance to us than they could ever have imagined. They give us an idea or direction that inspires us. They let us know that we are not alone.

Those of us who are graced with the com-panionship and comfort of a loving pet know that animals can be Angels, too. Pets can be there for us at just the right moment. Their joy at seeing us at the end of the day can lift a heavy heart, and remind us that we're needed and loved. Animals are Angels for a lot of people—the connections they can provide have been known to restore people to health or even give some a reason for get-ting up in the morning. Sometimes, the sud-den appearance of a hummingbird, a firefly or an animal in our backyard can bring a spark of magic to our lives.

Other Angels bring to us the artistic beauty we experience. Think about the

When you can love one tree or one flower or one dog or one place, or one person or yourself for one moment, you can find all people, all places, all suffering, all harmony in that one moment.
—JON KABAT-ZINN

As it is, these remain: faith, hope and love, the three of them; and the greatest of them is love.
—1 COR. 13:13

I've been a first-grade teacher for over twenty years. It's always been very important to me to create valuable growth experiences for my young students. I begin each new year with an orientation exercise in which the students stand up and tell what they want to be when they grow up. One student, Nancy, announced her intention to become a housekeeper just like her mother. It seemed, at the time, that Nancy had a very limited pool of options. Being a housekeeper was certainly a legitimate choice, but I wanted to make sure Nancy knew that it wasn't the only choice available to her. I made a personal commitment to help her realize a bigger, wider range of alternatives to draw from, so that her aspirations didn't come from a place of inevitable destiny. Two weeks before summer break, the first-graders repeated the exercise. Nancy stood up in the circle of chairs, stated her name proudly and said that she wanted to be a teacher!

—ANNA

There comes that mysterious meeting in Life, when someone acknowledges who we are and what we can be, igniting the circuits of our highest potential. I see this as the appearance of an angel, and know it to be a moment of Grace.

—RUSTY BERKUS

many authors whose books open our hearts, whose quotes hit us between the eyes or whose stories take us to enchanting places. Or consider the artist who creates drawings, paintings and images that capture a moment of beauty and can center us and remind us of who we really are. We can tune in to music for a burst of energy, a moment of relaxation or a flash of inspiration because of the gifts shared with us by songwriters, composers and musicians. And where would we be without those wonderful cooks and chefs who make our mouths water, who bring to us the essence of the garden and who often provide a medium for a special connection with others?

Many Angels in disguise come in the form of the loves of our lives. They are the children who reflect back our love for them, along with all the joy and hope we lavish upon them. They are family members whom we cherish deeply. They are the lovers of our soul and true being. They are the ones who bring tears to our eyes when we are truly in touch with how much we appreciate their presence in our lives. They inspire us, foster our creativity, make us smile, and laughingly and lovingly support our growth. They are our dearest friends, who reflect back to us the love we are capable of, the love we have in our hearts. As with all Angels in disguise, our spirits are enriched and sometimes forever altered because they have graced our lives.

Every blade of grass has its Angel that bends over it and whispers, "Grow, grow."
—THE TALMUD

To love for the sake of being loved is human, but to love for the sake of loving is angelic.
—ALPHONSE DE LAMARTINE

My friend Mary was driving home at 10 P.M. on a dark stretch of Alameda Avenue when her tire went flat. She pulled over and almost immediately, a car stopped and the driver offered to change the flat. Mary watched, amazed, as the driver reached around his seat and pulled his wheelchair out. Then he lifted himself from the chair to the ground and changed the tire, refusing Mary's offers to assist. He quickly changed the tire, placed his wheelchair in the car and drove off with a wave. Mary never even got his name and number to send a thank-you. He was truly her "Angel on Alameda."

—LISA CRAMER

As I stood in the checkout line, I noticed a little girl with magnificent, painfully solemn eyes. Two women who were with the child berated her mercilessly: "Christina, sit still!" "Christina, shut up!" "Stop that, Christina!" On and on they ranted. The child neither moved nor spoke. When the adults got busy putting the groceries onto the conveyor belt, I leaned over and whispered, "Christina! I'm your fairy godmother, and I know a secret. I want you to always remember this secret. No matter what anyone ever says or does to you, Christina, remember this: You are perfect just the way you are." Her reaction was immediate and dazzling. She began to smile. Her smile went all the way up to her eyes and into her soul.

—REBECCA ALLEN

ACTIVITIES

- Complete the following sentence with as many examples as you can think of: "I am truly grateful for the Angels in my life, including _____." Add to this list whenever you wish.

- Write the word "support." Set a timer for five minutes and without stopping to think or question your thoughts, write down any ideas that come to mind with regard to this topic.

- Before you go to bed, think of at least five contributions to your life made by Angels in disguise that day. Try this activity for a week. Add to the list whenever you wish.

- Identify five people who have touched your heart in a profound or unique way. Describe what they've done. (Consider the impact of family members, neighbors, friends, coworkers, strangers, TV personalities, or even characters in your favorite movie or book.) Add to this list whenever you wish.

- Make a list of people you respect most in your life. Identify what you value or appreciate in each one.

- Acknowledge your Angels. Write a thank-you note to someone who has been an Angel in your life, even if you do not plan to send it or can no longer get in touch, for whatever reason.

- Be an Angel to someone who needs it. Look for an opportunity to do one nice thing each week (or each day) that gives someone else joy.

- Make a deliberate attempt to acknowledge a kindness done to you or a job well done, even if it was expected or required by someone's job description.

When my mother was diagnosed with terminal cancer, three of her friends rushed to both our sides and offered every kind of help imaginable. During those last six months of my mother's life, they cooked for her, shopped for her, cleaned for her, sat with her, read to her, loved her from their souls and comforted me over the immeasurable loss we were all experiencing. They were my mother's angels, and they were mine, too. I still call them the *Tres Angelitas* and say a thank-you prayer for them every day.

—LYNN COLLINS

Hold a friend with both of your hands.

—NIGERIAN PROVERB

A real friend is one who walks in
when the rest of the world walks out.

—WALTER WINCHELL

- Describe a fairy godmother (or -father) you know.

- Describe an example of an animal or pet that served as an Angel for you.

- How have you been an Angel in disguise for someone else? In what other ways could you be an Angel in disguise for someone?

What we do not claim
remains invisible.
—MARIANNE WILLIAMSON

*It is the friends that
you can call up at
4 A.M. that matter*

—MARLENE DIETRICH

Planet Earth is a class-room and those who come to us are our teachers along the way.

—D. TRINIDAD HUNT

Angels can fly because they take themselves lightly.

—G. K. Chesterton

The purpose of the guide is not to point the way, but rather to encourage the seeker.

—SHOSHONA BLANKMAN

God couldn't be everywhere, so he invented mothers.

—YIDDISH PROVERB

*There is as much
greatness of mind in
acknowledging a good
turn as in doing it.*
—SENECA

*No matter
Who he is,
Holy or not,
Make his words your own
If they're true.*

—JAPANESE FOLK ZEN SAYING

We all biologically and energetically need to be in contact with a source of power that transcends human limitations and turmoil. We need to be in touch with a source of miracles and hope.

—CAROLINE MYSS

True heroism is remarkably short, very undramatic. It is not the urge to surpass others at whatever cost, but to serve others at whatever cost.

—Arthur Ashe

*Whenever you share love
with others, you'll notice
the peace that comes to
you and to them.*

—MOTHER TERESA

Every contact with every human being is an opportunity for growth and the fulfillment of desire—one has only to be alert to the opportunities through increased awareness.

—DEEPAK CHOPRA

Nobody sees Santa Claus, but there is no sign that there is no Santa Claus. The most real things in the world are those that neither children nor men can see.

—FRANCIS PHARCELLUS CHURCH

6

The Pleasures
of Service

*E*ach day we have numerous golden, rich opportunities to experience the gifts of giving, helping, offering kindness or support and
reaching out to others in our path. Seemingly inconsequential
actions—opening a door for someone, sharing a special smile or carry-
ing something for someone—can have a far greater impact than we
could ever imagine.

Service can manifest as a physical kindness, such as connecting
with a gentle touch or bringing a flower to a friend. You can experience the pleasures of service when you run an errand or make some
brownies for an elderly neighbor. Watch the relief you can provide
simply by offering to hold a baby for someone struggling through a
cafeteria line or by offering to give up your seat on the subway or bus.
Visit someone who is sick or dying, and you perform an act of monu-
mental courage and compassion.

Service can also take the form of an emotional connection. Look
into someone's eyes and open your heart to really listen as you ask,
"How are you doing?" Consider how enriching it can be to offer an
extra moment of attention to someone in a phone conversation.

From time to time, I still get panicky about old issues of financial security. I've found that the best way to get out of my poverty programming is to give some money away. Giving an extra-generous tip or making a donation to a cause or a person in need is a powerful prosperity affirmation. It's my way of recognizing, "This is old stuff. All is well. I trust."

—JOY

Purposeful giving is not as apt to deplete one's resources; it belongs to that natural order of giving that seems to renew itself even in the act of depletion. The more one gives, the more one has to give.

—ANNE MORROW LINDBERGH

All that we send into the lives of others comes back into our own.

—EDWIN MARKHAM

Reaching out to a person who is new or who is perceived as different can be an act of tremendous social justice, human compassion and connection. Being truly present in any interaction is a most gratifying and rewarding gift for all concerned.

Give someone a compliment and notice what happens—between the two of you, and within you. Experience the deep satisfaction that can come from taking the time to thank someone sincerely or acknowledging a kindness done to you. Reaffirm a connection by sending a card, a fax or an email to someone special. Share one of your favorite poems, stories or jokes to brighten someone's day.

Service can also take the form of spiritual giving. Perhaps at its most basic level, we can create spiritual connectedness by simply holding kind thoughts about someone. If you know people who are going through a difficult period, wishing them well can make an immense difference at this critical time. You can send them support, imagining them moving through this reality more easily or peacefully. Or consider the potential power of sending healing energy or a prayer when you see an accident or pass a person who is living on the street.

Our culture rarely promotes the practice of forgiveness or acceptance in the face of either deliberate or inadvertently hurtful behavior. And yet our willingness to move beyond automatic, reactive responses in a moment of challenge allows us to hold to

Lord, make me an instrument of your peace.
—ST. FRANCIS

Life's most persistent and urgent question is: What are you doing for others?
—MARTIN LUTHER KING JR.

No act of kindness, no matter how small, is ever wasted.
—AESOP

The house was full that Saturday evening with teenage boys having a sleepover when Dad called to ask if I'd take Mother gambling the next day. I declined, suggesting we plan it for the next weekend. My friend Martha called later that evening, and I told her of Dad's invitation. We laughed at the thought of fleeing a teenage party, but she became serious and encouraged me to go. The next morning my spouse also encouraged me by saying he'd tend the on-going party. I called Dad and told him I'd be there. Mom and I lunched, gambled, and the six or seven hours of driving together were filled with wonderful conversation. Mom's back was hurting so I rubbed it for her and tucked her in for the night before I left for home. Mom died that night. What special blessings I was given.

—MARCIA KONS

Even the merest gesture is holy if it is filled with faith.

—FRANZ KAFKA

our center, act with integrity, and serve more effectively and with a higher purpose. For example, holding a blessing in your heart for a driver who has cut you off changes what would otherwise be a stressful and negative event to an entirely different experience. Imagine the relief available when we are able to release a long-held grudge or forgive someone whose behavior we perceived with anguish, hurt or disappointment. Perhaps the most profound form of forgiveness comes when we can forgive ourselves, remembering that we have knowledge, strength and tools today that we may not have had in the past.

As you may well have experienced, there exists an inherent reciprocity, a give-and-take dynamic in the pleasures of service. Doing for others can provide a sense of your own well-being and connection with the world in particularly deep ways. Giving reinforces your foundation of trust, as what you give out comes back in most unusual, synchronistic ways. Generosity begets generosity. More often than not, the jar is not emptied, but replenished and replaced with an even bigger jar.

We can do no great things—only small things with great love.
—MOTHER TERESA

We must not only give what we have; we must also give what we are.
—DÉSIRÉ-JOSEPH MERCIER

I recently heard a story about a high-school girl who cele-
brated the first paycheck she received for an after-school
job. She took her aunt out for lunch at a local fast-food
restaurant and, at the counter, ordered three extra burgers
for a family of homeless people she had passed on the
street outside the restaurant. It seems that the previous
weekend at their prom-night dinner, she and a group of
her friends were surprised when they were told that their
expensive meals had been paid for by an anonymous
couple who were inspired by memories of their own prom
many years before. "I just had to pass the kindness on,"
the girl explained.

—Martin

Whenever I went anywhere with my grandmother, I
noticed how she would make it a point to say something
positive to the people she'd encounter. She'd always
acknowledge a friendly smile, pretty eyes, great service or
how beautiful a particular color looked on someone. She
had a remarkable ability to leave everyone she met feeling
uplifted or touched in some special way.

—Jane Bluestein

What's interesting about subscribing to a life of giving
is that you become addicted. It's a good addiction.
Once you get into the habit of reaching out to others,
you somehow always want to do more.

—Mary Kay Ash

ACTIVITIES

- Complete the following sentence with as many examples as you can think of: "I am truly grateful for the opportunities I have to serve, such as _____." Add to this list whenever you wish.

- Write the word "service." Set a timer for five minutes and without stopping to think or question your thoughts, write down any ideas that come to mind with regard to this topic.

- When you wake up tomorrow morning, remind yourself that you will have more than one special, unique opportunity to serve. Open your eyes wide, listen for that knock at your door.

- List ten gifts of service you could give now. (Remember that "gifts" do not have to cost any more than a smile!)

- List ten gifts of service you have received.

- List as many ways as you can think of that your job or work is contributing to your life and to the lives of others.

- Identify famous or well-known people that you admire for the gifts of service they offer others.

- Create a gratitude scrapbook for someone you love or admire. Include any of the following: photos, drawings, poems, comic strips, mementos, stories or a loving note about why you are grateful to have this person in your life. (You could also make a video- or audiotape to communicate your feelings for this person.)

- Identify those who richly serve you and the people you love.

- Clean out a closet or a drawer. Give away at least three things that someone else could enjoy.

- Smile at a stranger, give a compliment or offer some kindness to someone you don't know.

As you recall and recount the miraculous elements of life to others, you will be transformed personally. And you are actively delivering the invisible gifts of love, joy, peace, patience and kindness to others. In addition, you are delivering a foundation for hope.

—Glenna Salsbury

When you show your best face to the world and come from your highest level of integrity, you are serving others. . . . If your work is done with intention, consciousness and love, you are giving the most valuable contribution of all—you are adding light to the world.

—Sanaya Roman and Duane Packer

Thousands of candles can be lighted from a single candle, and the life of the candle will not be shortened. Happiness never decreases by being shared.

—BUDDHA

The fragrance always remains in the hand that gives the rose.

—GANDHI

*Guard well within
yourself that treasure,
kindness. Know how to
give without hesitation,
how to lose without
regret, how to acquire
without meanness.*
—GEORGE SAND

*If you contribute to other people's happiness,
you will find the true goal, the meaning of life.*
—THE DALAI LAMA

Even the thought of giving, the thought of blessing or a simple prayer has the power to affect others.

—DEEPAK CHOPRA

To receive more,
we must be willing to
give more. . . . It is
expressly at those times
when we feel needy that
we will benefit the most
from giving.
—RUTH ROSS

When confronted by small-mindedness, our task is to be part of the Light—to protect others, to stand up to others whose ideas are negative.

—CAROLINE MYSS

*We must be willing to
recognize and heal any
form of violence, poverty,
and imbalance within
ourselves as individuals
if we hope to eradicate
these problems from
our world.*

—SHAKTI GAWAIN

*On the days when I
feel love and compassion
and forgiveness in my
life, I'm happier and
more attractive to other
people.*

—MARIANNE WILLIAMSON

If I can put one touch of a rosy sunset into the life of any man or woman, I shall feel that I have worked with God.

—HENRY DAVID THOREAU

*When you get to
the very bottom of the
human soul—to the
place where the nit
slams up against the
grit and you're sinking
pretty bad—somehow
you manage to reach
down and help someone
who is sinking worse
than you are. Well,
that's when everybody
gets high and you don't
need any [substances]
and you don't need any
jewels or light. . . .
All you need is love.*

—Wavy Gravy

*Joy is a way of life. Joy
is magnetic, contagious
and productive, and is
perfect proof that giving
enriches the giver. As
joy pours out from me,
everyone is enriched,
including me.*

—DONALD CURTIS

*If I was going to exploit
my status as a person
who works in the movies,
it'd be tacky to keep the
money. People who have
been lucky are under
some obligation to help
people less lucky.
I certainly have
everything I need.*

—PAUL NEWMAN

Peace, joy and order are contagious. When they are present in you, they will spread into the environment that you are in, or that you pay attention to.

—BOB LANCER

*One of the greatest
ways you can help other
people is to speak forth
casual words predicting
good in their behalf.
Often you can mentally
accept good for others
that they have not yet
been able to mentally
accept for themselves.*

—CATHERINE PONDER

7

Silver Linings

*I*magine a world in which there were no unnecessary tragedies—not because negative events did not occur, but because we recognized that somehow these occurrences might have been necessary to open the way for some greater blessings to happen. One of the greatest challenges in life is learning to see the benefits of seemingly negative or tragic incidents. It takes a great deal of courage to reframe old hurts or violations in a positive light. Sometimes it may take years before a tragedy can make sense in this context or fit into a more positive perspective.

Even minor annoyances can sometimes generate grief, anger and feelings of victimization. Without questioning the value of processing any painful experience, it can help, at some point, to step back and see how these experiences can serve a greater, more positive purpose. We forget our checkbook when we are already running late and notice, when we irritably run back into the house, that the burner on the stove was not completely turned off. We narrowly avoid hitting another car and suddenly notice an increase in our awareness and attentiveness on the road. An illness forces us to reevaluate our priorities, habits and

In the middle of preparing the final version of the manuscript for this book, I received a phone call telling me that my brother had just died, very suddenly and unexpectedly. Because the memorial was going to be so small and private, and because I was in the middle of so many pressing deadlines, I had considered not making the long journey back home for the service. I thought I would stay where I was and take some personal time to process this event in the comfort of friends and private meditation. However, I made a last-minute decision to fly back to be a part of the family experience. I am forever grateful that I did. While I expected a brief and intimate gathering, I was overwhelmed by the numbers and diversity of the people who attended, by their openness and their raw vulnerability, and by the sense of community I witnessed. I did not realize the degree and the variety of ways in which my brother had touched so many people's lives. I could hear that these friends truly experienced and recognized the essence of who Jim Schmitz was. I gained an even greater appreciation for my brother. This experience also provided an opportunity for me to connect with family members in a deeper way, making closer connections as a result of the respect and love we shared for him.

—Judy Lawrence

In the darkest hour the soul is replenished and given strength to continue and endure.

—Heart Warrior Chosa

commitments, reminding us of the preciousness of every moment we have. A death or a loss brings greater connectedness and understanding among family members, communities or even nations.

Yet how many of us have the strength and commitment to resist the urge or conditioning to use our pain as an excuse to minimize demands made on us, to relinquish personal responsibility for choices we make, to gain attention or sympathy, or to justify vengeful actions? We are not happy that these painful events happened, but when we can view inconvenience—or even abuse or disaster—as part of a bigger picture, as an opportunity for growth and learning, we cease being victims who are powerless and vulnerable. For example, we are better able to stand up for ourselves, make our own decisions, and function confidently and independently after losing or leaving a controlling partner. We realize, often at the end of a long and exhausting process, that we are more aware and responsible for our own safety as a result of an accident or attack. We are more willing to take greater creative risks having experienced disappointment, embarrassment or failure—and having lived to tell about it. We use our reaction to criticism or insults to alert us either to behaviors we need to change, people we need to avoid or a craving for approval we need to examine. We are intensely and consciously more supportive, loving and nurturing to our children

At the bottom of the abyss comes the voice of salvation. The black moment is the moment when the real message of transformation is going to come. At the darkest moment comes the light.
—Joseph Campbell

The lowest ebb is the turn of the tide.
—Henry Wadsworth Longfellow

Change is inevitable. Growth is optional.
—Author Unknown

Month after month turned into year after year. My health was deteriorating. Each visit to a doctor or clinic resulted in a more bizarre medical test and another foreign-sounding diagnosis with a somber prognosis. At year four, I decided to go ahead with a much-wanted pregnancy. My third child was born just in time to start the new year. A few months after her birth, I finally received the correct diagnosis for my condition. Even though I was frustrated that it had taken five years, I was lucky the diagnosis did not come sooner, as I would have been strongly advised not to have any more children under these circumstances. Eighteen years later, that disease is in remission, and I have watched all three of my children grow up to become wonderful, caring adults.

—LILA

Our lives are not clear-cut paths to predetermined destinations. Things are always happening to us along the way. Our lives turn out to be a succession of surprises requiring mid-course corrections.

—CARL A. HAMMERSCHLAG

Love is the only prayer.

—MARION ZIMMER BRADLEY

as a direct result of early abuses we suffered and do not wish to repeat.

At a societal level, we see the existence of silver linings in the passage of more effective legislation and the development of safety procedures and products that often follow a catastrophic event. Consider the fact that the awareness and promotion of "random acts of kindness" emerged from frequent news references to "random acts of violence." We've been confronted with information and experiences that have forced us to rethink previously unquestioned behaviors and, in many cases, to make more conscious decisions about how we treat our bodies, interact with one another or impact the environment.

When we can believe that all things happen for the greatest good, we position ourselves to forgive, to release the burden of our pain and fear, and to be of greater service to ourselves and others. We stop hating ourselves for addictive or destructive behaviors that may have kept us alive until we had the strength and support to make more constructive choices. We celebrate a talent or interest we may not have uncovered had some life-changing event not forced us to slow down and let it surface. We see the strength and skills available to us only because of a loss we weathered. We see how our hearts have been opened by our grief, and know that our compassion, confidence and faith are gifts that linger in the wake of our anger and pain.

The challenge is to hold on in bad times. If you hold on tenaciously, I believe, the universe is on your side. When you know within yourself that sooner or later the wheel is going to turn your way, that somehow you will endure and persevere, then you have positioned yourself to grow and succeed.
—LES BROWN

When you get to your wit's end, you'll find God lives there.
—ANONYMOUS

When I was growing up, gratitude was used as a drug to get us to stop feeling anything that anyone perceived as negative. Anytime I was sad or angry about something, anytime I complained, I was invariably told that I should be grateful that things weren't worse. It took me years to realize that I could indeed be grateful and still, at times, feel disappointed, upset or annoyed, and even longer to learn how to let others be hurt or angry without telling them how lucky they were about something else!

—Lizzie

We are most often in the dark when we are the most certain, and the most enlightened when we are the most confused.

—M. Scott Peck

Clear away the wreckage of your past.

—Alcoholics Anonymous

ACTIVITIES

- Complete the following sentence with as many examples as you can think of: "I am truly grateful for the silver linings I've experienced in my life, including _____." Add to this list whenever you wish.

- Write the word "blessings." Set a timer for five minutes and without stopping to think or question your thoughts, write down any ideas that come to mind with regard to this topic.

- Describe how your life is better today than it was at some time (or various times) in the past.

- Describe a negative or hurtful event you personally experienced. Afterward, tell what you learned as a result of this experience, what you now understand or do differently, how your life is better now because of what you went through then.

- The next time you're feeling victimized, angry, resentful, alienated, disempowered or thoroughly frustrated, write about what happened to trigger those feelings. Use these feelings to explore how your own behavior or beliefs may have contributed to this incident and what you are willing to do differently in the future, either to prevent a recurrence of this event or in response if it happens again.

- Describe a way in which a past hurt (or hurtful experience) enabled you to help, nurture or support someone else.

- What positive local, regional, national or global changes do you see that have come about as a result of negative, tragic or disastrous events?

- What positive characteristics do you exhibit today that might not be a part of your character were it not for some painful event in your past?

As long as things are hunky-dory, people aren't going to change. Chaos and crisis can often be the catalysts for bringing people together, for building community.

—JACQUELINE CAMBATA

The I Ching teaches that the key to having a quiet heart is to give up resistance and accept where you are right now, no mattter how uncomfortable that place may be.

—CAROL OSBORN

In the end, there are no mistakes. There is only yearning and learning.

—DAN ZADRA

Your life is not a
problem to be solved
but a gift to be opened.
Just as the pain, hurt
and suffering that came
to you as a child were
powerfully real, so is
the tangible resilience
of your spirit equally
vital and alive.

—WAYNE MULLER

Biologically and spiritually we need to bring all things to closure. . . . After any painful and traumatic experience, we always receive internal guidance that can help us release the past and move on with our lives.

—CAROLINE MYSS

Chaos is creativity seeking form.

—DAWNA MARKOVA

There is no reason to linger around anyone who brings out the worst in you. Flee from them. Cast them out. Don't try to change them; change yourself, change friends.

—LES BROWN

Whenever you fall,
pick something up.
—OSWALD AVERY

You must lose a fly
to catch a trout.
—GEORGE HERBERT

*All through my life I
have attempted to turn
adversity into an ally.
And chaos into a
comedy. Sometimes I
succeed in spades.*

—Wavy Gravy

God gave burdens, also shoulders.

—YIDDISH PROVERB

There is no chain of
disasters that will not
come to an end.
—GEORGE S. CLASON

*It is not that there is
no evil, accidents,
deformity, pettiness,
hatred. It's that there
is a broader view.
Evil exists in the part.
Perfection exists in the
whole.*

—HUGH PRATHER

Endurance pierces marble.

—NORTH AFRICAN PROVERB

*Never fight the
darkness. Growth is
taking place. Let it.*

—CATHERINE PONDER

*It is a sad fact of life
that most people have to
lose a lot of data before
they get in the habit of
backing up their files.*

—DAVE

If your day isn't going well, start it over. Even if it's a minute before midnight, start it over. It's never too late.

—BIKER STEVE

8

The Gift of Perspective

*T*here's this great scene in the movie *Don Juan de Marco* in which the psychiatrist, played by Marlon Brando, challenges the perceptions of his patient, Don Juan (played by Johnny Depp): "What would you say to someone that said to you this is a psychiatric hospital and that you're a patient here and that I am your psychiatrist?" Don Juan replies, "I would say that he has a rather limited and uncreative way of looking at the situation." He goes on to say that he is not limited by his eyesight and that he sees beyond what is reasonable to the eye.

Acknowledging the gift of perspective is a wonderful way to highlight the blessings in your life. Sometimes perspective means noticing what is beyond the "reasonable eye," sensing the invisible behind the visible. If you've ever been snorkeling, you may remember the startling contrast between what you could see when you looked at the water from above and what appeared the instant you broke the surface with your face mask. Another unseen dimension is revealed through the lens. In the same vein, the popularity of the Magic Eye pictures seems to reflect our fascination with seeing beyond what is immediately obvious.

I recently witnessed a wonderful transformation in a friend who had been struggling with mediocrity in her life. Over a very brief period of time, she received a number of challenging work assignments that lasted over a year. During that time, she cut back on and finally stopped devoting Friday nights to recreational drinking with her husband. In addition to regaining the time she would have lost to all-day Saturday hangovers, my friend has also recovered her sense of accomplishment, motivation and excitement about her life. She is exuberant about retrieving a life she had nearly forgotten she had.

—Lisa

It is never too late to be what you might have been.

—George Eliot

Once you've learned to welcome change, adapting to it becomes a lot easier than resisting it.

—Craig R. Hickman and Michael A. Silva

As we develop the gift of perspective, we become better able to accept on faith many things for which we previously needed good, solid evidence. Think of those special people in your life you may not have heard from in quite a while. Perhaps today you realize that this lack of contact—concrete "evidence" of the bond between you that was once necessary to sustain your faith in the friendship—does not diminish the feelings they still hold for you.

In other areas of your life, you may now be open to possibilities that never would have entered your reality before. Perhaps you are willing to consider alternatives in thinking, being or manifesting that you may once have dismissed as ridiculous or impossible, had these thoughts even occurred to you at all. How do you see yourself in relation to the rest of humanity? How has your sense of interconnectedness developed over the years?

Look at the development of your relationship with yourself. Are you willing to examine facets of your personality that would have scared you off in the past? Are you more accepting of your own vulnerability and imperfections? Perhaps today you are more willing to reacquaint yourself with aspects of your being you may previously have denied. The emergence of your authentic self is a testament to your compassion and courage in this area.

Success is going from failure to failure with great enthusiasm.
—WINSTON CHURCHILL

The past does not have to equal the future.
—ANTHONY ROBBINS

Today I consciously forgive myself for my past mistakes. I give thanks for the lessons they have taught me, and I move forward to a greater expression of life.
—WILLIAM T. CURTISS

I recognized the man who had his hand on his son's shoulder. The man softly explained why he was buying him the tape player as I was writing up the sale. The loving scene triggered a painful memory. Sixteen years ago, when this man and I attended the same junior high, he had attacked me because I had walked into his neighborhood. I had done nothing to provoke him; I had simply entered a place in which he felt I didn't belong. But now I maintained my "salesman politeness," thanking him for the sale. As he left, I felt confused. For years, I had fantasized about reciprocating the beating and getting back at him. But now I saw him as a loving father, someone who is polite to other adults. This was a moment of growth and calming in my soul.

—JERRY TERESZKIEWICZ

You do not get out of a problem by using the same consciousness that got you into it.

—ALBERT EINSTEIN

The past is over. Wipe the dirt off your feet.

—MARIANNE WILLIAMSON

If you have been changing gradually, you may not have realized or acknowledged how much your perspective has changed and how well your new perspective is serving you now. For example, have you noticed a softening in your attitude regarding your ability to accept others? Are you less judgmental than you used to be? Are you less rigid about how things have to be done at work, at home, with your kids or in your adult relationships? If your perspective about your family history or long-standing personal issues has changed, you realize that new doors are now open for the present and future to flow in more fully.

Look at the way you deal with emotions and attitudes today. Are you now able to handle setbacks, disappointments or frustration with greater ease, grace, wisdom, confidence and personal responsibility? Perhaps you are less reactive today, more open to other people's perspectives. Maybe you take things less personally. Consider how your approach to your friends, your work, your lifestyle or the demands of change is different from earlier attitudes or patterns. In what ways are you more deliberate about the options you consider and the choices you make?

Your perspective affects more tangible aspects of your life as well. For example, when you think about finances, you may recognize changes in your patterns or thinking. When you spend money, do you now stay conscious, spending with priorities

Some people are always grumbling because roses have thorns. I am thankful that thorns have roses.
—ALPHONSE KARR

Just behind the visible world is a whole other world in which it all works differently.
—RAM DASS

I'm not a professional, not hardly. I just like to take pictures and I usually do a pretty good job capturing the spirit of the occasion. I tend to experience an event very differently when I'm behind a camera. In a way, I'm a little less a part of what's going on, but everything around me is somehow more focused and real. Through the lens, I see details I would not ordinarily notice. I'm more aware of people's energy and personalities as I wait for the ideal moment to record not only what they're wearing or that they're having a great time, but who they are. Without the camera, it's just a great party. And that's okay. But I love the shift in awareness and perspective that the camera affords me.

—ANTONIO

Being on your path is what it's all about. Each destination you reach only opens out into wider horizons, new and undiscovered countries for you to explore.

—BARBARA SHER

and values in mind instead of simply trying to fill an inner emptiness? Are you loosening up and letting go of the fear of being penniless, spending the money you do have more comfortably? What's your spin on abundance these days?

The gift of perspective covers a lot of ground. Think of the many ways your present beliefs, behaviors and attitudes reflect changes in your perspective. Use these pages to record these special insights.

In the dark
I lost sight of
My shadow;
I've found it again
By the fire I lit.
—JAPANESE FOLK ZEN SAYING

Years ago, when I was facing a severe crisis in my life, a very important friend advised me to take care of myself. "You sound really fragile right now," he cautioned. I was devastated. He could not have attached a more accusatory, insulting or terrifying label. Fragile! After a lifetime of hiding behind a façade of tough competence, strength and independence, I felt betrayed and exposed by my own vulnerability, a part of myself long disavowed. Yet in this moment began the long and painful process of reacquainting, retrieving and reconciling scattered and lost pieces of who I was, of coming home to myself, of becoming whole.

—ALEX

Love and kindness are here all the time, somewhere, in fact, everywhere. Usually our ability to touch them and be touched by them lies buried below our own fears and hurts, below our greed and our hatreds, below our desperate clinging to the illusion that we are truly separate and alone.

—JON KABAT-ZINN

ACTIVITIES

- Complete the following sentence with as many examples as you can think of: "I am truly grateful for the gift of perspective as it is reflected in _____." Add to this list whenever you wish.

- Write the word "perspective." Set a timer for five minutes and without stopping to think or question your thoughts, write down any ideas that come to mind with regard to this topic.

- Select one of the topics in the list that follows (or identify a topic of your own). Tell how your perspective has changed with regard to the particular topic over the past five, ten, fifteen or more years. Topics may include: love, relationships, friendship, health, money, work, children, your body, humanity, nature, abundance, spirituality, family, joy, fun, success, learning, power, wisdom, compassion, connectedness, play, obligation, responsibility, integrity and self-care. Repeat this activity with as many topics as you wish.

- List people, resources (books, tapes) or experiences that have influenced your perspective in some way. Describe the impact each has had on you.

- Describe how changes in your perspective have been gifts in your life.

- Notice people around you and watch for people with a perspective you admire or may want to adopt. In your writing, tell what it is about their perspective that pleases you and what similarities of perspective you may already have.

- Ask your close friends to remind you of three examples of significant growth or personal development in you that they have observed and admired in the last five or ten years.

- Describe how your life is better than you ever expected it to be.

- Tell how your life is better than that of previous generations (your parents' lives, for example).

- Reflect on the best choice you ever made. Review the situation. What made the option so clear?

What though the radiance which was once so bright
Be now forever taken from my sight,
Though nothing can bring back the hour
Of splendor in the grass, of glory in the flower;
We will grieve not, rather find
Strength in what remains behind. . . .

—WILLIAM WORDSWORTH

*Developing any higher
quality—be it love,
inner peace, well-being,
happiness, courage,
personal power or self-
respect—will change
your vibration and
make you magnetic to
whatever matches your
new vibration.*
—SANAYA ROMAN AND
DUANE PACKER

*Trust that you will
never repeat [the] same
mistakes again, but
please allow yourself
the freedom to make
new mistakes and
learn new lessons.
All has value.*
—SINDA JORDAN

Error is only the opportunity to begin again, more intelligently.
—HENRY FORD

*Patient waiting is often
the highest way of
doing God's will.*

—JEREMY COLLIER

Have faith that you can trust your own happiness.

—CAROL OSBORN

In times of pain,
when the future is too
terrifying to contemplate
and the past too painful
to remember, I have
learned to pay attention
to right now. . . . In the
exact now, we are all,
always, all right.

—JULIA CAMERON

In virtually all of the great spiritual and philosophical traditions of the world there appears some form of the idea that most human beings are sleepwalking through their own existence. Enlightenment is identified with waking up.

—NATHANIEL BRANDEN

*The good news is
that no matter what
happened in the past
we are not bound by
previous patterns,
seeming failures,
emotional responses or
health challenges.
The unchanging, invin-
cible principles of truth,
love, wisdom and joy
triumph over prior
experience. Today we
can make a 180-degree
turn in any area of our
lives we want to change.*

—SAGE BENNET

*As you learn to live
from your intuition,
you give up making
decisions with your
head. You act moment
by moment on what you
feel and allow things to
unfold as you go.*

—SHAKTI GAWAIN

The only reality there is, is what we tell ourselves.
What we believe, we become.

—RUTH ROSS

We are now old enough
to quote ourselves.
—SJ SANCHEZ

If you have to be someplace other than where you are, you'll never see the here and now.

—CARL A. HAMMERSCHLAG

You can't make a wrong choice. . . . You can't possibly miss your life's calling. No matter what you're living, it's serving your life.
—CAROLINE MYSS

The highest spirituality is to have a great sense of humor and appreciation for the absurd.

—NANCY KNICKERBOCKER

I do not seek to understand that I may believe,
but I believe in order to understand.

—ST. ANSELM OF CANTERBURY

The world needs sane
people. You can no
longer afford the luxury
of your fear of
uncertainty.

—TARA SINGH

*Listen! There is a song
for every soul that plays
like a fountain at the
heart of every life.
Listen to your own life
song. Be ever sensitive
to her calling. When
you are caught in the
storms of life, her sweet
silver sound will lead
you home.*

—D. TRINIDAD HUNT

9

A Pat
on the Back

*M*ost of us have busy and challenging lives filled with family responsibilities, work projects, school events, religious involvements, community commitments, and obligations to keep our pets and plants alive. So much of our life is consumed with such routine and ordinary tasks that it's easy to feel invisible and lose sight of how much we actually accomplish in a day. On top of that, it may seem silly or self-indulgent to actually give ourselves recognition for the everyday activities that occupy our time.

How often do we forget to give ourselves a pat on the back for the things we do? How often do we fall asleep haunted by unfinished items on our daily to-do lists? A first step might involve simply listing a number of tasks you finish in the course of a day. If nothing else, stopping to acknowledge progress and accomplishments can help reframe our focus from what we're *not* doing to what we actually do achieve. A simple pat on the back can encourage, validate, reinforce, strengthen and empower, especially when we begin to doubt the purpose and progress of our actions and intentions.

Here is a place to record constructive choices you make, examples

A few years ago, I took time off to travel. On my trip, I gradually learned to quit controlling every aspect of my life and to trust instead, letting each day unfold. On one adventure, I was following a friend's rather complex directions to get to her uncle's home where I was to stay a few days. I left Athens on Easter Sunday and traveled by train to a small town in the north. From there I took a taxi through the country, past a factory to the next gas station on the right. Her note directed me past a "mad, barking dog," up a hill to a fenced area. All was going according to plan until I saw the lock on the fence. But even though I was out in the middle of nowhere in a foreign country on a holiday weekend, locked out of the place I was supposed to go, it never occurred to me that I wouldn't be okay. I somehow knew this would all work out. I climbed the fence and walked through the trees. Eventually I found a small house and knocked—no answer there or at the next house. But at the third and last building, I knocked and there was my friend's uncle! I ended up having a wonderful visit and an even stronger sense of trust.

—Judy Lawrence

When we know who we are and are comfortable with ourselves, we can live clearly and courageously.

—Wayne Muller

of personal integrity, courage and deter-mination, and times you've demonstrated the self-discipline to follow through on commitments you've made to yourself and others. Which of your many talents, skills and resources have you recently utilized or shared?

Start tracking some of the more mean-ingful accomplishments in your life. For example, after endless years of study, do you finally have the degree you wanted? Have you finished cleaning the garage after months of annoying reminders in the back of your mind? Did you finally sign up for the French class, tap dance lessons or com-puter instruction you had been putting off for years? Let yourself know what a good job you did. Any small step you take toward achieving a big goal or vision deserves recognition.

How about acknowledging the times you successfully used restraint when deal-ing with your children, spouse, family members, coworkers or neighbors after a particularly bad day? Did you resist the temptation to ground your child for the rest of his life? Were you able to take a ten-minute breather instead of instantly blasting your secretary about all the errors you just found in an important report? What about other times you took advantage of a chance to work through your feelings instead of reacting or taking them out on others?

By the same token, think of the times you stood up for yourself, set a boundary or

Don't ever let anyone tell you that there's anything wrong with self-congratulation.
—Barbara Sher

Compliments are gifts of prosperity. Learn to accept them graciously.
—Louise L. Hay

It takes more courage sometimes to face our greatness than it does to face our weakness.
—Marianne Williamson

Finances were never my strong suit, but when my husband and I decided to get some help with our budget, I saw my whole self-esteem take a turn for the better. As instructed, I started tracking my spending every day. A curious pattern started to show up in a very short time. I could see that whenever I was having a bad day, the first thing I would do was go out for a latte and chocolate croissant. Now there certainly are times when this is the perfect comfort and solution for me; however, after watching the pattern and noticing my feelings, I realized that what I really wanted was to feed my inner self more than my body self. From then on, when I wanted to feel better, I went to a special art supply store instead. Now when I spend my money, I feel like I'm feeding my inner self, and I'm so pleased with myself when I do.

—Dana

We can always rely on the fact that there is a wisdom within us that knows everything. It always knows the answers we seek, the solutions to our problems, the choices we need to make, all of which will lead to greater inner peace, grand creativity and more opportunities to express and experience our majestic inherent nature.

—Linda McNamar

asked directly for something you wanted, despite the possibility of rejection, anger or being ignored. Have you been working on inner personal growth issues for a while? Sometimes just having the courage to look within and be with your true self deserves a major pat on the back. Add to that the faith it took during those times when you trusted your instincts or absolutely surrendered and let go of your need for control. You may imagine those decisions were no big deal, yet deep down you know what a big deal they were. There was probably a time when these actions would have been impossible for you, had they even occurred to you in the first place. Write down what an incredible job you did and give yourself an extra pat on the back for your fearlessness. (Give yourself two extra pats if you were afraid and still did it anyway!)

It is time to finally notice all of the incredible and worthwhile things about yourself, despite any messages from the past that discouraged self-accolades. That was the past, where self-care was confused with selfishness and self-confidence with conceit. Now it's time to toot your own horn, to appreciate who you are and to value your contributions to the world. Pat yourself on the back! Congratulate yourself for a job well done! Use these pages to practice giving yourself recognition that is both well-deserved and probably long overdue. It's okay to be recognized. It's okay to be visible. And it's definitely okay—

When you are struggling with a problem, fighting to fend off the bullets, you forget about all the experiences, resources and wisdom you've been collecting all your life. . . . You already have the inner resources to construct a way through.
—DAWNA MARKOVA

Trust in yourself. Your perceptions are often far more accurate than you are willing to believe.
—CLAUDIA BLACK

When I first met Gene, he was wearing a bandage where his left middle finger and index finger should have been. I found this especially tragic since he was a cabinetmaker. But he was upbeat, almost jovial. He told me that as a child, his grandfather had told him to do every activity both right- and left-handed so that he would never be unable to work. After only a month of healing, Gene was back designing and building cabinets just as before. He was as happy and productive as ever, since he didn't let this setback get in his way.

—JERRY TERESZKIEWICZ

Who you are is a necessary step to being who you will be.

—EMMANUEL

The greatest gift you give others is the example of your own life working.

—SANAYA ROMAN AND DUANE PACKER

if not essential—to know you truly deserve this attention, especially from yourself.

Blessed are those who can please themselves.

—Zulu proverb

ACTIVITIES

- Complete the following sentence with as many examples as you can think of: "I am truly grateful for the gift of accomplishment as it is reflected in _____." List your accomplishments here. You can use this activity to acknowledge daily tasks you complete (for example, what you crossed off your to-do list today), examples of character development or the achievement of significant lifetime goals. Add to this list whenever you wish.

- Write the word "success." Set a timer for five minutes and without stopping to think or question your thoughts, write down any ideas that come to mind with regard to this topic.

- Describe three of the most significant or satisfying accomplishments of your life. Then go back and do the same for the past year, the past month and the past twenty-four hours.

- Make a list of things you can do now that you could not do five years ago; ten years ago; twenty years ago. In addition to specific skills or accomplishments, consider improvements in, for example, your ability to set boundaries, trust yourself, acknowledge your achievements or demonstrate your courage.

- Make a collage of images that represent things you can do well.

- Write a love letter to yourself.

- Ask your close friends to remind you of three examples of your characteristics, talents or accomplishments they admire or appreciate.

- Make a list of things you could do that would feel like great rewards for yourself. (See if you can come up with two dozen examples or more!)

- Identify five to ten areas of your life that are important to you, such as family, creativity, your work, your body, physical health, spiritual well-being, community, your home, friends, emotional balance, time management, learning, communicating, day-to-day issues, play or relaxation, or other priorities. List your skills, competencies and attributes in each area.

- Make a list of ten positive adjectives that describe yourself. Give an example of each one.

- Describe something that once felt threatening or overwhelming that no longer frightens or holds power over you.

Be grateful for your guilt. This uncomfortable mental state is giving you the gift of realizing that however brilliant and justified your rationalizations, even you aren't buying them.

—Carol Osborn

Be able to be alone.
Lose not the advantage
of solitude, and the
society of thyself.
—SIR THOMAS BROWNE

Eliminate something superfluous from your life. Break a habit! Do something that makes you feel insecure.

—PIERO FERRUCCI

*God is something inside
of us that believes in
ourselves.*

—José Affonso F. Barbosa

Each and every one of us wants to be the best that we can be! Every soul wants to be a great human being. Every soul sets out with the best of intentions.

—D. Trinidad Hunt

Life is made of moments.
Find yours.
—VOICESTREAM

ADVERTISEMENT SLOGAN

*If ants are such busy
workers, how come
they find time to go to
all those picnics?*

—MARIE DRESSLER

*The greatest self-help technique you can practice
is the art of laughing.*

—DIANA LUPPI

Although you keep
A jewel within yourself,
Nobody will notice it
Unless you
Polish and brighten it.
—Japanese folk Zen saying

Try not to get caught up in needing to have an immediate answer. . . . Inner guidance seldom gives us long-term information; it usually just lets us know what we need in the moment.

—SHAKTI GAWAIN

*Do not worry about your difficulties in mathematics;
I can assure you that mine are still greater.*

—ALBERT EINSTEIN

*The only reality there is,
is what we tell ourselves.
What we believe, we
become.*

—RUTH ROSS

Self-care is an attitude of mutual respect. It means learning to live our lives responsibly. It means allowing others to live their lives as they choose, as long as they don't interfere with our decisions to live as we choose.

—MELODY BEATTIE

*He who knows others
is learned. He who
knows himself is wise.*

—LAO-TZU

*Anger is meant to be
listened to. . . . Anger is
meant to be respected.
Why? Because anger is
a map. . . . Anger
points the way, not just
the finger.*
—JULIA CAMERON

I think I can,
I think I can.

—*The Little Engine That Could*

10

The Miracle
in the Mirror

$\mathcal{A}$s you review all the gifts in your life for which you are grateful, have you remembered yourself? This chapter is where you can acknowledge one of the greatest gifts of all—*you,* just the way you are, the miracle in the mirror.

Now it's time to appreciate the real you, not just the job you do, the clothes you wear, the car you drive, or the parent, child, spouse, boss, employee or neighbor you represent for someone. It's time to recognize and cherish that unique, loving, dependable, interesting, capable, caring and intriguing person who greets you in the mirror every morning. It's also time to acknowledge your love for every single aspect of that beautiful being beaming back at you in the mirror.

If you suspect that this type of positive focus and self-recognition may be frivolous, self-centered, conceited, inappropriate or simply impossible, you're certainly not alone. For many people, attempting to describe oneself in positive terms can be excruciatingly difficult, painful or embarrassing. Many of the messages we have received throughout our lives have been critical: focusing on flaws, disappointments and inadequacies. Some of us have even been taught that

There I was in my closet, my hand on the skirt I'd relent-lessly held onto since high school. The last time I had worn it was twenty years—and twenty-five pounds—ago. It wasn't even in style anymore! But somehow, every time I had gone through my wardrobe, I'd stubbornly passed by this outfit, imagining that one day I'd surely be able to wear it again. I looked down at my body—my soft, round body that looked so great in the other clothes I owned—and realized that this skirt's day was long past. It was with great joy that I realized I no longer even felt the need to wear this skirt, or change the shape of my body to allow it to fit once again. I was fine the way I was. I put the skirt in the give-away basket. Perhaps someone else could wear it and enjoy it as I once had.

—OLIVE

You begin to change the moment you love yourself
for being the way you are.

—GAY HENDRICKS

Remember to remember who you are and why you're here.

—D. TRINIDAD HUNT

feeling good, proud or happy tempts fate, bringing some personal catastrophe as retribution! So naturally, voluntary self-criticism—even to the point of deflecting a genuine compliment—may come far more easily.

A simple exercise—saying to yourself "I love you exactly the way you are" at various times throughout the day—can be a bridge for accepting those features, flaws and characteristics that always seemed unacceptable in the past. Start by finding the one thing you can honestly say you love or appreciate about yourself. Maybe you have a great smile, beautiful hair, a terrific sense of humor, a strong handshake or a sexy voice. Eventually move on and start to love the you beyond the cellulite or wrinkles. (It may be easier for you to start with "I accept you exactly the way you are" or "I acknowledge you exactly the way you are.")

Another way to begin is by taking a moment to thank your body for the ways it takes such good care of you. How often do we even think about our automatic ability to breathe or the fact that our heart is beating whether we're thinking about it or not? For some of us, taking the time to notice and value the most basic elements of how our body functions is necessary to overcome the negative conditioning many of us experienced.

Are you going through life with a minimum of colds, flus, various illnesses, ailments or hospital stays? Are you physically able to do

You'll never be able to dance unless you hear your own music.
—CARL A. HAMMERSCHLAG

Always be a first-rate version of yourself, instead of a second-rate version of somebody else.
—JUDY GARLAND

Each Life is an original work of art. When are you going to start signing autographs?
—RUSTY BERKUS

My son was born two months premature. During the next several months, he would scream furiously and unmercifully. It seemed that his digestive system was not developing correctly. When I took Paul to the pediatrician for an examination, I was told that the problem had been found: "You need Valium," the doctor said. I promptly walked out and found a solution on my own.

—SJ SANCHEZ

Everything you will ever need may be found within your own body, heart and spirit. Your most difficult task is to believe in yourself.

—WAYNE MULLER

Just remember, you don't have to be what they want you to be.

—MUHAMMAD ALI

most of the things you want to do? Often we don't appreciate our ability to walk up a set of stairs until we have a foot or leg injury. We take washing our hair for granted until we have a cast on our hand or arm. If you're not feeling particularly healthy at the moment or have a history of illness, can you step back and appreciate your body's ability to heal, the parts of your body that *are* healthy, or the things you are still able to do in spite of your illness or disability? Can you embrace your potential for healing and picture yourself functioning at optimal health at some later point in time?

As you continue to acknowledge that miracle in the mirror, keep in mind your other personal qualities, which represent the authentic you and reflect your inner beauty—your patience, wisdom, strength, generosity, integrity, creativity, kindness, intuitiveness, fearlessness or courage, for example. Which of these have you utilized well during your life so far?

Perhaps it is easier for you to be grateful for your intellectual talents. What are your strongest skills in this arena? Are you a whiz at analyzing, problem solving, organizing or delegating? Do you have a talent for creating order out of chaos, simplifying the complex or making the impossible possible? Can you organize your thoughts and communicate clearly? Sometimes it's hard to see skills that come easily to us as the magnificent assets they are.

Examine the special qualities you have

We're so engaged in doing things to achieve purposes of outer value that we forget that the inner value, the rapture that is associated with being alive, is what it's all about.
—JOSEPH CAMPBELL

Why become a Buddhist when you can become a Buddha? We're all Buddhas by nature, and it's incumbent on us to become all that we are.
—SURYA DAS

"What is *real?*" asked the Rabbit one day. "Real isn't how you are made," said the Skin Horse. "It's a thing that happens to you. When a child loves you for a long, long time, not just to play with, but really loves you, then you become Real. . . .Generally, by the time you are Real, most of your hair has been loved off, and your eyes drop out and you get loose in the joints and very shabby. But these things don't matter at all, because when you are Real you can't be ugly, except to people who don't understand."

—FROM *THE VELVETEEN RABBIT* BY MARGERY WILLIAMS

We must choose—sometimes against seemingly impossible odds, with enormous evidence to the contrary—to love whatever we encounter.

—PETER MCWILLIAMS

You need not apologize for being brilliant, talented, gorgeous, rich or smart. . . .Your playing small serves no one. . . . Stop it immediately. Come home to the castle.

—MARIANNE WILLIAMSON

shared with those around you. What other traits and skills do you think you may have to offer that are still buried deep inside you? Acknowledge the unique contribution you have made to the world, simply by being a one-of-a-kind miracle that exists nowhere else on earth.

A friend is a gift you give yourself.

—ROBERT LOUIS STEVENSON

ACTIVITIES

- Complete the following sentence with as many examples as you can think of: "I am truly grateful for the following things about myself: _____." Add to this list whenever you wish.

- Write the word "self." Set a timer for five minutes and without stopping to think or question your thoughts, write down any ideas that come to mind with regard to this topic.

- Make a collage of images that represent your most positive personal attributes.

- Write about the miracle of who you really are, keeping in mind the physical, emotional, intellectual, creative and spiritual sides of you.

- Make a list of the last several compliments you received. Which qualities or talents do others recognize most frequently? Which comments seem most congruent with what you already believe about yourself? Which ones seem most inconsistent with what you have learned or felt about yourself? Which ones surprised you the most?

- Notice how you respond when someone gives you a heartfelt compliment. Are you able to take it in without feeling embarrassed or apologetic, and without ignoring, dismissing or minimizing what they have shared with you? (Try saying "thank you" and see what happens.)

- Call yourself at home and leave a loving message on your voice mail or answering machine.

- Ask your closest friends to share with you one or more qualities they appreciate and value most in you.

- Wearing your favorite, most flattering clothes, stand in front of the mirror and look at yourself. Notice at least five comfortable or pleasing aspects about how you present yourself to the world.

- Stand in front of a mirror without your clothes on and notice five positive, wonderful and satisfying features or attributes that are represented by what you see.

- List several qualities you think may be buried deep inside of you.

- List the admirable qualities you truly value in others and consider how they reflect similar qualities in you.

- Reflect on the word "essence." Ask yourself, "What is my essence?" Write down your response. Review your writing and revise it as often as you like.

*My health . . . seems to be the by-product of a life lived full-bore.
I set out to forgive myself and others totally. I set out to obey the
passions of my art. I chose work as my talisman. As a by-product
of these choices, I found myself healing.*

—CANCER SURVIVOR JOE KOGEL

Use what talents you possess: the woods would be very silent if no birds sang except those that sang best.

—HENRY VAN DYKE

When we look with our hearts, and not with our eyes, we can see beauty in all things.

—JANE BLUESTEIN

*Perfection already is. It
is up to us to perceive
perfection in the sun-
shine, in the shadows,
in the conflict, in our
own progress, and in
life's ever-changing
appearances. We do
not have to strive to
be perfect; we need to
realize our divine
perfection right now.*
—SAGE BENNET

Live your life and
forget your age.
—NORMAN VINCENT PEALE

The only way to acquire that feeling of security is to enter the whirlwind of change and come out the other end, feeling alive again.

—CAROLINE MYSS

*Here in this body are
the sacred rivers: here
are the sun and moon,
as well as the pilgrimage
places. I have not
encountered another
temple as blissful as my
own body.*

—SARAHA

*Personal power is not
aggressive, muscular,
manipulative or authori-
tative power, but an
inner power that comes
from knowing we have
all the resources we
need to handle whatever
happens in our life.*

—Ruth Ross

*I can live for two
months on a good
compliment.*

—MARK TWAIN

*The right voice is one
that's not scolding, one
that does not make us
feel guilty. It's a voice
that encourages us to
use the gifts that we've
been given, to use them
well, and to use them
for a contribution to the
world and to all life in
the world.*

—MERLIN STONE

Always know in your heart that you are far bigger than anything that can happen to you.

—DAN ZADRA

All you need to know
is already inside you
waiting to be received.

—SINDA JORDAN

*Be faithful to that
which exists nowhere
but in yourself.*

—ANDRÉ GIDE

Drifting in a sultry day
on the sluggish waters
of the pond, I almost
cease to live and begin
to be.

—HENRY DAVID THOREAU

11

Wish List

*T*he genie is out of the bottle. You have three wishes—and the third wish is always an automatic wish for three more! There is more abundance and magic available to us than we can ever imagine, let alone use in one lifetime. Our lives are a stream of endless actions that often begin as wishes. Imagine the possibilities if all good things start as wishes—conscious or unconscious! We all have desires, for ourselves and for others. Whatever blessings we now have in our lives began as wishes from somewhere.

But sometimes even wishing can be a bit frightening. Have you ever limited your wishful thinking because you believed you could never really have what you wanted, or weren't sure you deserved to receive all that you dared to wish for? Have you ever feared that your receiving might deprive someone else, or set you up for some negative backlash? Does the potential for being disappointed or having to wait too long keep you from opening the door to the endless and wonderful possibilities you would truly wish for yourself?

The good news is that scarcity and limitations in our thinking are learned behaviors; they can be unlearned. We can make a deliberate shift to focus on abundance, limitlessness and infinite opportunities.

My massage therapist was going through an extremely difficult time. The time she spent at the hospital bedside of a daughter and granddaughter who had been critically injured in an auto accident prevented her from working and earning her living. I wanted to help her out and decided to prepay for a block of sessions. I debated between five sessions and ten, and decided to stay with my first impulse and pay for ten sessions, although it seemed like a lot of money at the time. A week later, I received a letter back from her thanking me and telling me her story. On the long drive back home from the hospital, she calculated the expenses she would need to cover in the next few days. The gravity of her situation became apparent when she realized that she needed gas to get home and was down to ashtray change. She figured she needed $400 to meet her immediate bills and keep her utilities turned on. She pondered several options and finally decided to surrender the problem and turn it over to God for help. When she got home, she stopped to pick up her mail and found her box overflowing. There was one envelope that did not look like a bill. When she opened it, there was my check for $400—exactly what she needed!

—GUADALUPE

It is astonishing how short a time it takes for very wonderful things to happen.

—BARBARA SMALLWOOD AND STEVE KILLBORN

Our wishes affirm our faith and optimism, and help to turn us in directions in which we want to move.

Many of our wishes are for material things: burning desires and longings for specific "goodies," like getting a car, adding to our CD collection or acquiring that new, hot, fashionable piece of clothing. Do you find yourself wishing for a new pair of Rollerblades, a flashier computer or more closet space? Desires for mundane, every-day commodities can be a good place to start because the path to fulfilling these wishes is often easily identified, the achievement is tangible and quantifiable, and the changes required in our behavior or beliefs may be relatively minimal.

Notice other areas of your life that you desire to be different. What financial goals are you seeking? Do you aspire to a zero balance on your credit card bills, a bulging piggy bank, a down payment for your first home or an easy, comfortable retirement? What about emotional wishes, such as peace with one of your family members or the ability to deal with a personal trauma and finally release it once and for all? Socially, you may be seeking out deeper, richer friendships, genuine connections or the relationship of your dreams. Psychologically, your goal may be freedom from old, self-defeating beliefs and habits. Or perhaps you may wish for greater physical health, fitness or energy than you are currently experiencing.

The water does not flow until the faucet is turned on.
—Louis L'Amour

What if you do, indeed, get to have it all?
—Maurine Renville

You are never too old to set another goal or to dream a new dream.
—Les Brown

One day, after deciding I needed to take a particular computer class, I was looking at the continuing ed catalog and reading the course description. I knew that I needed this class, but I was concerned with how much it cost. As I was sitting at my desk, trying to decide how I was going to work this class into my schedule and budget, the phone rang: It was an offer for a free computer class at this new learning center that had just opened in town. It was the exact same class I had just been reading about! I learned that this offer was part of a marketing effort to let people know about this center. I signed up, had a great class and saved $150 in the process.

—JUDY LAWRENCE

You are never given a wish without also being given the power to make it true.

—RICHARD BACH

Things happen when the time is right—when we're ready, when God is ready, when the world is ready. Give up. Let go. But keep it on [the] list.

—MELODY BEATTIE

Our wishes may also include a desire for greater spiritual connectedness, a willingness to surrender and accept guidance, or opportunities to be of greater service. Many of our wishes go far beyond our own needs and desires. They may include a prayer for the health of our children, a wish for the success of a friend or the desire for a peaceful resolution to some national conflict. When we get down to these nitty-gritty wishes, don't they somehow reflect the profound yearnings that make us reach for our essence, for the depth of compassion, for the love in our souls, and for the passion to experience the goodness and full enjoyment of our lives?

We each embody a source of fulfillment, a wishing well that is deep and rich. Each wish taps into an enormous pool of possibilities that truly does exist. How often are you dipping into your wishing well? Why not more often? Do you go to the well with a thimble, or do you hook up a pipeline? After all, there's plenty there! Make your wishes and then let go. Regardless of your past experiences or prior beliefs, it's possible to make all sorts of wishes, or believe in all sorts of possibilities, without being attached to specific outcomes.

We're not starting from ground zero—we've been making wishes all along. Notice how many have already come true, including wishes that allowed for greater fulfillment by *not* coming true! Our wishes may not manifest in the exact form we initially

Whatever you can do or dream you can do, you can. Boldness has a genius, magic and power to it.
—GOETHE

I have lived to thank God that all my prayers have not been answered.
—JEAN INGELOW

You must begin by knowing you have already arrived.
—RICHARD BACH

I love my new house up near the mountains on the edge of the city. However, after I moved, I missed the close views I used to get of the hot-air balloons that fill our skies during our annual Balloon Fiesta, and frequently lamented the fact that the balloons never made it up to this end of town. The other night, coming in from taking out the trash, I saw what I thought was the moon, nearly full, a pale glow in the clear night sky. But wait! This "moon" was moving, and it was moving fast! A balloon in this neighborhood? At night? Impossible! I looked up, and there were six or seven others, drifting toward the canyon, glorious against a black sky and backdrop of stars. These were the gas balloons, off on a race across the country, something I had never seen before. It took my breath away. I went up and down my street, ringing all my neighbors' doorbells to let them in on the magic. In the two years I'd lived in this house, I'd never actually met many of these people. What a nice way to finally connect—and what a surprising way to get my wish!

—CHELSEA

You can ask for anything. . . .Start with the assumption that you can get what you want.

—JACK CANFIELD AND MARK VICTOR HANSEN

imagined we wanted. (Have there ever been times when something better came into your life when a wish didn't come true?) Sometimes our wishes simply lead us to other wishes we may not realize we have.

We have the ability to attract and create what we want in our lives, even though the route to our desire may not be direct, immediate or particularly obvious. Use your wish list to help identify goals and desires, to shape a direction for future choices, and to acknowledge wishes that have already been granted. Often, pursuing your wishes takes personal courage, willingness, patience and faith. Wishing connects you to your true passion on your life's journey. So go ahead—dream the dream, vision the vision and wish the wish!

In some form or other, every desire reaches its goal. . . . Let go of the desire. You don't have to mail a letter twice; just know that the message was delivered and your result is on the way.

—Deepak Chopra

ACTIVITIES

- Complete the following sentence with as many examples as you can think of: "I am truly grateful for the power of possibilities as it is reflected in my desire for _____." Add to this list whenever you wish. (Alternate: "I am truly grateful for the following wishes that have already been granted: _____.")

- Write the word "imagine." Set a timer for five minutes and without stopping to think or question your thoughts, write down any ideas that come to mind with regard to this topic.

- Identify five to ten areas of your life that are important to you, such as family, creativity, your work, your body, physical health, spiritual well-being, financial abundance, community, your home, friends, emotional balance, time management, learning, communicating, day-to-day issues, play or relaxation, or other priorities. List goals, plans or desires in each area. (Or make a collage to represent your goals, plans or desires.)

- Write about past wishes, wishes you made at different stages in your life. Which ones came true?

- Tell how your life benefited from a wish *not* coming true. What greater need or desire was fulfilled in its place? In what ways is your life better? Are there any other wishes that did not come true for which you are grateful?

- Having made your wish list, how are you living your life in gratitude until your wishes are fulfilled?

- Identify examples of abundance that already exists in your life.

- What wishes do you have for others?

- How would your life be different if you had everything you wanted?

Ask, and it shall be given you; seek and you shall find; knock, and it shall be opened to you. For everyone who asks, receives; and he who seeks, finds; and to him who knocks, it shall be opened.

—MATT. 7:7, 7:8

Sometimes the most direct route to success appears to go in exactly the opposite direction from where you intend to go.

—CAROL OSBORN

*While you're on your
way to your pot of gold,
don't forget to pick up
the silver along the way.*

—Author Unknown

*It is very difficult to be
clear about what you
want when your mind
is overwhelmed by input
about what you're
supposed to want.*
—MARIANNE WILLIAMSON

Just let go. Let go
of how you thought
your life should be,
and embrace the life
that is trying to
work its way into
your consciousness.
—CAROLINE MYSS

Now when I awaken
and before I even open
my eyes, I thank the
bed for a good night's
sleep. After all, we have
spent the whole night
together in comfort.
Then with my eyes still
closed, I spend about
ten minutes just being
thankful for all the good
in my life. I program
my day a bit, affirming
that everything will go
well and that I will
enjoy it all.

—LOUISE L. HAY

Never think that God's delays are God's denials. Hold on; hold fast; hold out. Patience is genius.

—Comte Georges Louis Leclerc de Buffon

Often our spending differs from our real values. We fritter away cash on things we don't cherish and deny ourselves those things we do.

—JULIA CAMERON

*Some things . . .
arrive on their own
mysterious hour, on
their own terms and
not yours, to be seized
or relinquished forever.*
—GAIL GODWIN

Chance is always powerful. Let your hook be always cast; in the pool where you least expect it, there will be a fish.

—OVID

*Take the time to know
what it is you want. In
order to choose well, we
have to know our true
desires. Many of us
have been so busy
attending to others
that we haven't allowed
ourselves the quiet to
attend to our own
inner stirrings.*

—JOAN STEINAU LESTER

Asking is one half of the mantra, the other half is being willing to receive. Listen and be ever alert, for when the universe answers, it may be in the language of little synchronicities that guide you toward a solution. Ask knowing that an answer is forthcoming. Then be ever alert to catch it.

—D. Trinidad Hunt

The creative life force, or energy of the universe, flows through you and literally connects you to all-that-is. Through your attention, or focus of thought, you draw the specifics unto you.

—JERRY AND ESTHER HICKS

If we're having trouble feeling grateful for what we have, maybe a good place to start is feeling grateful for what we don't have: all the miseries and sorrows that—for the moment—have passed us by.

—PETER MCWILLIAMS

12

The Joy
of Creation

For some of us, the word "creativity" conjures up images of the irresistible invitation of a blank canvas, a mass of unshaped clay or a blank notebook and a new pen. For others, it is the music waiting to be discovered in the touch of a harp, horn, piano, drum or violin. Still others may see it as the promise and possibilities in a bag of unspun wool, a tube of colorful beads, a burl of wood or a slab of marble. Every day presents an opportunity to make something new, to bring to life something that does not yet exist.

Yet creativity is not limited to those who are good with their hands or their imaginations. The term also applies to the creations that come through our hearts, our kindnesses and our positive thoughts. Simple things we do in the course of a day are far more creative than we may ever imagine. Being efficient and functional with our time and our space is a form of creativity, too. For example, we create order in our lives anytime we straighten up a room, sew a button, glue a broken pot, rebuild an engine or pay our bills on time. Our creativity may be evident in the furnishings we assemble to make our homes more beautiful or the combination of clothes we select to create feelings

Some time back, I was observing a friend's painting. I have always been in awe of people who can create pictures from a blank canvas and actually make it recognizable. I can't! I expressed to my friend how much I'd always wished I was creative, and she looked at me like I'd just fallen out of a tree. She smiled tolerantly at me and said, "What about your writing? What about your work? What about the hundreds of ways I see you be creative?" I realized, through her eyes, what a narrow perspective I had on true creativity. I actually thought of it only as the artistic things I cannot do. How could what I do easily and regularly be creative? Her questions set me to wondering how many other forms of creativity I miss. I now know myself as an enormously creative person . . . who doesn't paint very well.

—LYNN COLLINS

If you do not already have a Creative License, we suggest you apply for one immediately. We assure you it will come in very handy as you try to accomplish what it is you came here to do.

—DIANA LUPPI

of comfort, confidence, attractiveness or power. It may be present in the meals we cook, in the way we maximize limited space or in a unique approach to a stubborn problem.

You don't need to be an artist to create warmth, reassurance or connectedness with your smile. If you can't weave a basket, weave a story. If you can't create a sculpture, use your arms to fashion a hug. Tie a ribbon in a child's hair, put a flower in a windowsill vase, weed your garden or pick up some litter, and you add a little to the beauty in the world. You can soothe a broken heart with the music in your soul, whether in a symphony you compose or the harmony of a soft and understanding voice.

Open your heart and summon your gentleness to create comfort and shelter for a hurt or tired child. Provide emotional safety through your listening, acceptance and love. Inspire aspirations with your encouragement and faith. Instill a sense of competence with your patience and your willingness to demonstrate, teach, answer a question, provide a resource or celebrate an accomplishment. Allow your own curiosity, enthusiasm and explorations to create space for someone else to take a risk or try something new. All of these gestures reflect enormous creativity!

Create joy by writing a letter or visiting an isolated friend. Tell a joke and create laughter. Give freely and create abundance for yourself and others. Call a friend to share a

Every artist dips his brush in his own soul, and paints his own nature into his pictures.
—HENRY WARD BEECHER

One can never consent to creep when one feels an impulse to soar.
—HELEN KELLER

Life shrinks or expands in proportion to one's courage.
—ANAÏS NIN

The relationship I had been in for a number of years was dissolving. At the end of this relationship, I decided to clear out an old, cluttered shed on the back right corner of my property. It was suggested by a *feng shui* professional one year prior that if I wanted a better relationship, I should straighten out this shed. As I was cleaning and clearing, I recited the affirmation, "I release that which no longer serves me, and I allow into my life miracles and magic." I started ripping stuff off the walls and pulled away an old piece of carpet that was covering a window facing out over the ravine. In the window was a sign that warned "Keep Out!" In the twenty years I had been in the home, I had never realized that the sign or the window were there. I ripped up the sign as a symbol of allowing a relationship into my world, just as the uncovered window allowed light into the shed. I had Sheetrock and carpeting installed, planted flowers and put a "Welcome" sign on the door. Shortly after, I was in a new relationship, one that was more supportive, richer and respectful than I ever could have imagined.

—CAROL

In the province of the mind, what one believes to be true either is true or becomes true.

—JOHN LILLY

rainbow or sunset you just noticed, and another heart may sing. Say a kind word or a prayer for someone and feel the energy you create. Release an old hurt, and create forgiveness and reconciliation. Kindness creates kindness, and love creates love. And anytime you can resist using criticism, judgments, discouragement, sarcasm, ridicule, comparisons or perfectionism—in dealing with yourself and others—you avoid injuring a creative spirit.

Create a sense of self-appreciation and personal worth by taking some time for yourself, practicing healthy choices, getting a massage, taking a quiet walk or avoiding negative people. Create space for "new and better" by cleaning out a closet, letting go of a worry or fear, accepting a loss or disappointment, or leaving an unfulfilling relationship. Let the world see your growth and recovery, and somewhere you can create hope or direction for someone in pain. Live large and live well, and your confidence and success can create inspiration. Live in great gratitude for who you are and what you have in your life, and you can create optimism and peace of mind.

Given all these opportunities, we can hardly help but create. If you've ever claimed to be hopelessly uncreative, it may be that you haven't yet had the safety, support, encouragement or opportunities to allow your creativity to fully emerge, or perhaps you've been limiting your sense of what creativity can entail. Use these pages

You win some, you lose some, and some get rained out, but you gotta suit up for them all.
—J. ASKENBERG

Our goal while on this earth is to transcend our illusions and discover the innate power of our spirit. We are responsible for what we create, and we must therefore learn to act and think with love and wisdom, and to live in service to others and all of life.
—CAROLINE MYSS

Each spring in the small villages of northern New Mexico, three mission churches in tiny communities are selected for a restoration project. The whole community joins together and totally embraces the project. The community hosts volunteers from many surrounding towns as well as relatives who have returned for the occasion. Talented carpenters come out and use their expertise and creativity with such heart and soul. Women who remember the training from their grandmothers apply the adobe plaster with their hands. And great cooks serve the most delicious meals, as full of tradition and love as one could ever imagine.

—Sam

Cherish your visions; cherish your ideals; cherish the music that stirs in your heart, the beauty that forms in your mind, the loveliness that drapes your purest thoughts, for out of them will grow all delightful conditions, all heavenly environment; of these, if you but remain true to them, your world will at last be built.

—James Allen

to note and affirm the wonderful ways you create each day. For in the end, our creativity will be best reflected in the life we create from the life we were given. We are each an essential and imperative part of the creative process, wizards in our potential for creating magic, miracles and synchronicity for ourselves and for others whose hearts we touch.

Look at life through the windshield, not the rear-view mirror.

—CAROL MARKS

ACTIVITIES

- Complete the following sentence with as many examples as you can think of: "I am truly grateful for the gift of creativity as it is reflected in _____." Add to this list whenever you wish.

- Write the word "creativity." Set a timer for five minutes and without stopping to think or question your thoughts, write down any ideas that come to mind with regard to this topic.

- Describe ways in which you are creative.

- Take an hour or two to go someplace that's visually exciting for you—perhaps an antique store or a vintage clothing store, a hardware or an office supply store, a museum, a greenhouse or nursery, a pet store or crafts supply house. Notice new ideas or creative uses for the different things you see that are sparked by being in this stimulating environment.

- Make a list of things you've made recently.

- Describe how your creativity is apparent in the order, beauty and functionality of your home or work environment.

- Describe how your creativity is apparent in your relationships and the ways in which you interact with others.

- Describe any progress you have made in your efforts to avoid impairing creativity in yourself or others (for example, by avoiding criticism, perfectionism, judgments, impatience, disappointment, comparison or discouraging remarks). Note: Simply noticing any tendencies you may have in this area is progress.

- Describe how your creativity helped you turn a negative experience into a prosperous, satisfying, enriching or favorable outcome.

- What are some new ways in which you can express your creativity?

To laugh often and much; to win the respect of intelligent people and the affection of honest critics, and endure the betrayal of false friends; to appreciate beauty; to find the best in others; to leave the world a bit better, whether by a healthy child, a garden patch, or a redeemed social condition; to know even one life has breathed easier because you have lived: this is to have succeeded.

—RALPH WALDO EMERSON

*I believe in therapy. But
if I'd waited for it to fix
me up, I'd have been
ninety before I walked
out the door. . . . You
can spend years under-
standing your fear of
water and still never
walk to the edge of the
pool and jump in.*

—BARBARA SHER

When we, as individuals, grow in consciousness, the mass consciousness shifts accordingly. As the mass consciousness changes, it pulls along other individuals who may be clinging to old patterns, or who are simply unaware of how to proceed.

—SHAKTI GAWAIN

He who has a why to live can bear most any how.
—FRIEDRICH NIETZSCHE

*It is better to know
some of the questions
than all of the answers.*

—JAMES THURBER

*Rejoice in the
abundance of being
able to awaken each
morning and experience
a new day. Be glad
to be alive, to be
healthy, to have
friends, to be creative,
to be a living example
of the joy of living.*

—LOUISE L. HAY

*You do not feed a seed
continually. You feed it,
then give it time to
absorb, digest and
develop a new need for
more nourishment. It
must be the same with
your efforts. Do not
drown your new plant.
Work on it, then let it
go . . . over and over.
Rhythmically, patiently.*

—BOB LANCER

Your own
Self-Realization is
the greatest service you
can render the world.

—SRI RAMANA MAHARSHI

*Part of the passion
that urges us to create,
to display, to tell our
story, is the passion of
divine revelation itself.
Divinity is seeking to be
revealed everywhere.*

—MATTHEW FOX

Vision and patience
help you integrate your
skills. While vision
helps you invent an
excellent future,
patience allows you
to take the necessary
time to implement it
successfully.
—CRAIG R. HICKMAN AND
   MICHAEL A. SILVA

*The more you say,
"I relinquish control, I
don't know how to do
this," the more energy
will come in. As you get
out of your own way, it
will become easier and
easier. All you need to
do is intend.*

—BARBARA MARCINIAK

*When you have a dream
and you recognize it as
something you can
actually strive to
realize, I believe life
opens up and offers
opportunities.*
—LES BROWN

What you are living today is as a result of the thoughts and feelings that you have felt before this. Your future is created from your perspective of today.

—JERRY AND ESTHER HICKS

To affect the quality of the day, that is the highest of arts.

—HENRY DAVID THOREAU

EPILOGUE

A Final Perspective

*I*magine there is a bank that credits your account each morning with $86,400, carries over no balance from day to day, allows you to keep no cash balance, and every evening, cancels whatever part of the amount you had failed to use during the day. What would you do? Draw out every cent, of course!

Well, everyone has such a bank. Its name is *Time.* Every morning, it credits you with 86,400 seconds. Every night it writes off, as lost, whatever portion of this amount you failed to invest to good purpose. It carries over no balance. It allows no overdraft.

Each day, it opens a new account for you. Each night, it burns the records of the day. If you fail to use the day's deposits, the loss is yours. There is no going back. There is no drawing against tomorrow. You must live in the present on today's deposits. Invest it so as to get the utmost in health, happiness and success! The clock is running. Make the most of today.

To realize the value of one year, ask a student who has failed his exam.

To realize the value of one month, ask a mother who has given birth to a premature baby.

To realize the value of one week, ask an editor of a weekly newspaper.

To realize the value of one day, ask a daily-wage laborer who has ten kids to feed.

To realize the value of one hour, ask the lovers who are waiting to meet.

To realize the value of one minute, ask the person who has missed the train.

To realize the value of one second, ask a person who has survived an accident.

To realize the value of one millisecond, ask the person who has won a silver medal in the Olympics.

Treasure every moment that you have! And treasure it more because you shared it with someone special, special enough to have your time. And remember, time waits for no one.

—*AUTHOR UNKNOWN*

This story appeared in *Lightbearer* 4 (July/August 1997):4–5.

Gratitude Groups

Although this book was originally conceived for individual use, as it developed and emerged, its usefulness in a group setting became increasingly obvious. If you wish to use this book as a basis for group meetings or activities that focus on gratitude, consider the following guidelines and suggestions.

LEADERSHIP

In some cases, gratitude groups will be started, coordinated or facilitated by a teacher, counselor or other group leader. In others, groups may simply represent a number of friends, associates or community members who come together to explore various dimensions of the topic as it applies to their lives.

If your group does not have a leader or facilitator, you will probably want to determine, as a group, whether or not you want to have some form of leadership and, if so, what form that leadership will take. Decide whether you want the same leader for each meeting or whether you'd prefer that group members take turns leading the group, either on a voluntary or rotation basis.

Identify the role or function the leader might assume. Duties may include:

- Keeping to the topic
- Starting and ending on time
- Reminding members about confidentiality

- Making sure that everyone who wants to share gets to share
- Introducing, explaining or suggesting activities to do in the group or between meetings
- Promoting and building acceptance and safety; reminding members to avoid interrupting, criticizing or judging other members' contributions, or attempting to give other members unsolicited advice

SCHEDULE AND LOCATION

We recommend a twelve-week meeting cycle, with each week (or meeting) devoted to one of the twelve chapters in this book. Of course, you can structure longer or shorter cycles, depending on the group's desires or interests. You may want to schedule a block of meetings and request a commitment from each member to participate in the entire twelve-week program if possible. Or you may wish to run an ongoing group over the course of several months or a year, inviting people to start at any point in the cycle and come whenever they wish.

Identify where these meetings will occur. Unless a specific meeting place has already been determined, you may wish to discuss the members' preferences for meeting in one particular location each week or rotating locales, meeting at members' workplaces or homes, schools, libraries, community centers, or in rooms made available through various retail or religious organizations.

Another approach may be to use a retreat schedule, either as a way to launch a longer cycle or to explore all twelve chapters (or selected chapters) in a one- to three-day format. You may also wish to have a meeting cycle culminate in a retreat to celebrate and review what happened during the course of this cycle. You can use a retreat center or resort, ranch, hotel, lake cabin or beach house, or someone's home or apartment. It doesn't have to be fancy—just a warm, inviting and comfortable place for people to bond and share.

Regardless of the format you choose, we recommend printing a schedule of dates and topics, especially for ongoing groups in which the cycle will repeat over and over.

OPERATION

Other considerations include deciding on the following:

- How long you want your meetings to be
- Whether to have snacks or refreshments and, if so, whether food will be brought on a bring-your-own basis, as a potluck for everyone to share or as a rotating responsibility
- Whether to have music during writing or other activities and if so, what kind
- Whether to limit sharing time and, if so, how
- Whether meetings will be closed to all but participants or open to guests and visitors

You will also need to address how you want to use the time you spend in and out of your groups. Feel free to use the activities in this book, either individually or as a group, providing time to discuss the experience. In addition to discussing the topics or doing the activities in each chapter of this book, you may want to make time to discuss whatever members feel comfortable sharing, such as blessings, insights, challenges, intuitive moments, creative bursts, service projects, a new appreciation for themselves, positive experiences or the wondrous gifts that have entered their lives.

Your group may also decide to take on a particular project as a group activity. For example, your group might identify someone in the community (local or global) to acknowledge. Send this person a collection of expressions of appreciation from members in the group. Consider a group service project to undertake during holiday seasons—or at any time of the year. You might identify and share resources—books, tapes or videos, for example—to explore and discuss as a group, or identify speakers you may want to invite.

At the conclusion of the cycle, decide whether you wish to continue meeting, and, if so, how you can each maintain an attitude of gratitude, and how individual members can start groups of their own.

Angel Certificates

Here are certificates you can complete and pass on to the Angels in Disguise in your life. Feel free to duplicate these certificates and share them abundantly.

A Special Thank-You to an Angel in Disguise

This certificate acknowledges

_____

as an Angel in Disguise. A special thank-you for:

_____

_____

Your kindness and thoughtfulness are appreciated.

Signed _____ Date _____

A Special Thank-You to an Angel in Disguise

This certificate acknowledges

_____

as an Angel in Disguise. A special thank-you for:

_____

_____

_____

Your kindness and thoughtfulness are appreciated.

Signed _____ Date _____

A Special Thank-You to an Angel in Disguise

This certificate acknowledges

_____

as an Angel in Disguise. A special thank-you for:

_____

_____

_____

Your kindness and thoughtfulness are appreciated.

Signed _____ Date _____

A Special Thank-You to an Angel in Disguise

This certificate acknowledges

_____

as an Angel in Disguise. A special thank-you for:

_____

_____

_____

Your kindness and thoughtfulness are appreciated.

Signed _____ Date _____

A Special Thank-You to an Angel in Disguise

This certificate acknowledges

_____

as an Angel in Disguise. A special thank-you for:

_____

_____

Your kindness and thoughtfulness are appreciated.

Signed _____ Date _____

Service Certificates

On the following pages you will find certificates you can complete and pass on to someone to whom you wish to promise some gift of service. Examples of service you might consider offering include:

- Running an errand
- Baking someone's favorite goodies
- Preparing and delivering a casserole or some soup
- Providing a few hours of day care or baby-sitting
- Organizing a closet, a box of recipes or a photo album
- Helping to clean out a garage, attic or shed
- Helping to pack or move
- Helping to paint, wallpaper or put up shelves
- Weeding someone's garden or mowing someone's lawn
- Watching and caring for someone's pets or plants
- Treating someone to an afternoon at the movies (or renting a video)
- Teaching someone how to use new software
- Washing someone's car or changing the oil
- Returning library books
- Partnering for a walk, bike ride, racquetball game, board game or card game
- Sharing a day at the museum or aquarium
- Hauling trash or recycling for someone
- Braiding, coloring or cutting someone's hair

- Providing company on someone's next shopping trip (or doing that person's shopping yourself)
- Bringing someone flowers from your garden
- Doing a chore someone really hates to do
- Walking someone's dog
- Inviting someone for dinner at your house
- Taking someone's kids for a few hours (to a movie or playground, for example)
- Giving someone an hour of your time just to sit and listen
- Making a difficult phone call or drafting a letter for someone
- Helping with a challenging project
- Taking someone out for ice cream or coffee (or both!)
- Lending someone an article of clothing, an appliance or power tool
- Offering to pray, meditate, light a candle or hold a good thought for someone
- Hosting a party, shower or celebration for someone
- Making a contribution in someone's name to a charity of that person's choice

Feel free to add to this list and to duplicate these certificates and share them abundantly.

A Gift of Service

This certificate entitles

to the following gift of service:

Signed _____ Date _____

A Gift of Service

This certificate entitles

to the following gift of service:

Signed _____ Date _____

A Gift of Service

This certificate entitles

to the following gift of service:

Signed _____

Date _____

A Gift of Service

This certificate entitles

to the following gift of service:

Signed _____ Date _____

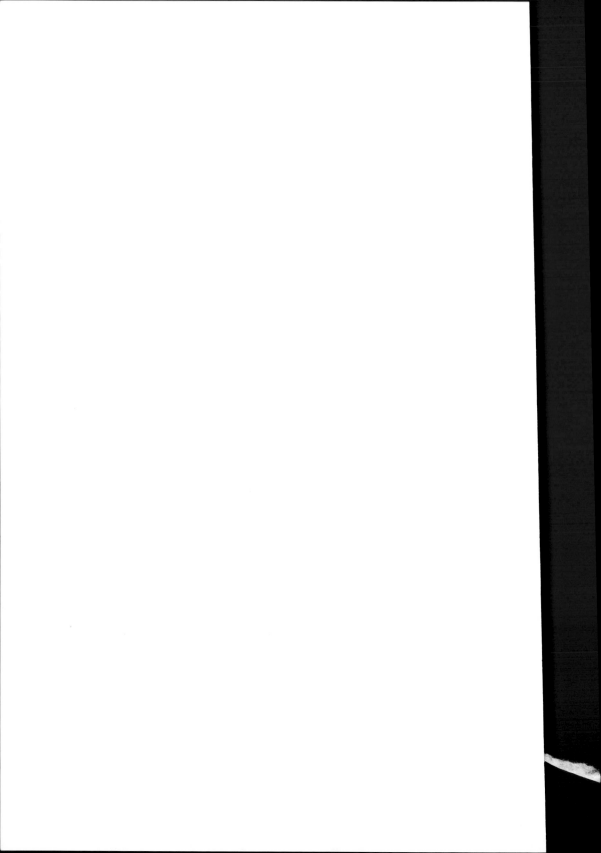

Let Us Hear from You

Do you have a gratitude story you'd like to share? We'd love to hear from you and invite you to share your experiences, observations or insights with us. We're also interested in learning about how you've used this book and the ways in which it has had an impact on you.

Please send your correspondence to us in care of:

Daily Riches
1925 Juan Tabo NE, Suite B-249
Albuquerque, NM 87112-3359
fax: 505-323-9045
email: *jblue@wizrealm.com*

Many thanks!

A World of Thanks

Expressions of Gratitude
from Around the World

Thank you
English

Efharistó
Greek

Hvala
Serbian

dhanyavaad
Hindi

Takk
Icelandic

Gratias
Latin

Spasibo
Russian

Xie xie
Mandarin

Diolch
Welsh

Dzię, kuję
Polish

Mahalo
Hawaiian

Dakujem vám
Slovak

Ke a leboha
Sesotho

Gracias
Spanish

Mulţumesc
Romanian

Asante
Swahili

Hvala
Slovene

Tack
Swedish

To-siä
Holooe

Köszönöm
Hungarian

terima kasih
Malaysian

Mercé
Occitan

Gràcies
Catalan

Arigato
Japanese

Merci
French

Shokran
Arabic

TODA
Hebrew

ngiyabonga
Zulu

Ďyakuyu
Ukranian

Cám ởn
Vietnamese

Eskerrik asko
Basque

Dhanyabad
Bengali

Hvala
Croatian

Danke
German

Ačiū
Lithuanian

Dank u
Dutch

Blagodarya
Bulgarian

Salamat
Tagalog

Kiitos
Finnish

A dank aych
Yiddish

Dankie
Afrikaans

Te sekkürler
Turkish

Terima kasih
Indonesian

Takk
Norwegian

Go raibh maith agat
Irish

Tak
Danish

Obrigado, Obrigada
Portugese

Dankon
Esperanto

Grazie
Italian

Děkuji vám
Czech

Tänan
Estonian

Kam-sa-ham-ni-da
Korean

_____

[*EDITOR'S NOTE:* In order to be consistent, all phrases have been set in Latin alphabetic characters.]

© Dr. Michael C. Martin, President, The travlang Company

3469 Cortese Circle, San Jose, CA 95127

(408) 251-5355 • *president@travlang.com* • http://www.travlang.com/

References

We gratefully acknowledge the following sources of many of the quotes we've used in this journal. Every effort has been made to identify the actual sources of the material and to secure the appropriate permissions wherever necessary.

Alcoholics Anonymous. New York: Alcoholics Anonymous World Services, 1976.

Allen, James. *As a Man Thinketh.* Marina del Rey, Calif.: DeVorss & Co.

Allen, Paul W., and Joan deRis Allen. *Francis of Assisi's Canticle of the Creatures: A Modern Spiritual Path.* New York: Continuum Publishing Co., 1996.

Allen, Rebecca. "A Modern Day Fairy Godmother." *The Light,* August 1997: 29.

Ash, Mary Kay. *Mary Kay: You Can Have It All.* Rocklin, Calif.: Prima Publishing, 1995.

Bartlett, John. *Bartlett's Familiar Quotations.* Ed. Emily Morison Beck. Boston: Little, Brown & Co., 1980.

Beattie, Melody. *Codependent No More.* New York: Harper & Row, 1987.

————. *The Language of Letting Go.* New York: Hazelden/Harper & Row, 1990.

Bennet, Sage. "Daily Guides to Richer Living." *Science of Mind* 69.11 (November 1996): 55, 63, 66.

Berkus, Rusty. *Life Is a Gift.* Encino, Calif.: Red Rose Press, 1982.

Boorstein, Sylvia. *It's Easier Than You Think.* San Francisco: Harper San Francisco, 1995.

Branden, Nathaniel. *The Six Pillars of Self-Esteem.* New York: Bantam Books, 1994.

Brown, Les. *Live Your Dreams.* New York: Avon Books, 1992.

Bruno, Dave. *Gold Card Collection.* Greendale, Wis.: Dave Bruno and Associates, 1996. 800-870-4410.

Cameron, Julia. *The Artist's Way.* New York: Jeremy Tarcher/Putnam, 1992.

Canfield, Jack, and Mark Victor Hansen. *The Aladdin Factor.* New York: Berkeley Books, 1995.

Carman, Bliss, ed., *The World's Best Poetry: The Granger Anthology,* 1st ser., vol. 4. Great Neck, N.Y.: Granger Book Co., 1981.

Catholic Family Edition of the Holy Bible. New York: John J. Crawley & Co., 1953.

Chandler, Mitzi. *Gentle Reminders for Co-Dependents.* Deerfield Beach, Fla.: Health Communications, 1989.

Chopra, Deepak. *Ageless Body, Timeless Mind.* New York: Harmony Books, 1993.

————. *Creating Affluence.* San Rafael, Calif.: New World Library, 1993.

————. *The Seven Spiritual Laws of Success.* San Rafael, Calif.: Amber-Allen Publishing, 1994.

Clason, George S. *The Richest Man in Babylon.* New York: Signet/Penguin Books, 1955.

Curtis, Donald. "Daily Guides to Richer Living." *Science of Mind* 70.7 (July 1997): 30, 62.

Curtiss, William. "Daily Guides to Richer Living." *Science of Mind* 70.6 (June 1997): 61.

Daleo, Morgan Simone. *The Book of Dreams and Visions.* Charlottesville, Va.: Grace Publishing & Communications, 1996.

Dukas, Helen, and Banesh Hoffman, eds. *Albert Einstein, the Human Side: New Glimpses from His Archives.* Princeton, N.J.: Princeton University Press, 1979.

Eisen, Armand. *A Little Book of Angels.* Kansas City, Mo.: Ariel Books/Andrews & McMeel, 1995.

"A Final Perspective." *Lightbearer* 4: (July/August 1997): 4–5

Fishel, Ruth. *Time for Joy: Daily Affirmations.* Deerfield Beach, Fla.: Health Communications, 1988.

Fox, Matthew. *The Reinvention of Work.* San Francisco: Harper San Francisco, 1994.

Gawain, Shakti. *Living in the Light.* Mill Valley, Calif.: Nataraj Publishing, 1997.

————. *The Path of Transformation.* Mill Valley, Calif.: Nataraj Publishing, 1993.

Gillies, Jerry. *Moneylove.* New York: Warner Books, 1978.

"God Moments." *Unity Magazine,* May 1996: 19.

Gravy, Wavy. *Something Good for a Change.* New York: St. Martin's Press, 1992.

Green, Jonathan. *A Dictionary of Contemporary Quotations.* New York: William Morrow & Co., 1982.

Griswold del Castillo, Richard, and Richard A. Garcia. *César Chávez: A Triumph of Spirit.* Norman, Okla.: University of Oklahoma Press, 1995.

Hammerschlag, Carl A. *The Theft of the Spirit: A Journey to Spiritual Healing with Native Americans.* New York: Simon & Schuster, 1993.

Harvey, Andrew, and Anne Baring. *The Mystic Vision: Daily Encounters with the Divine.* San Francisco: Harper San Francisco, 1995.

Hawken, Paul. *Growing a Business.* New York: Simon & Schuster, 1987.

Hay, Louise. *You Can Heal Your Life.* Carlsbad, Calif.: Hay House, 1984.

Hendricks, Gay. *Learning to Love Yourself: A Guide to Becoming Centered.* New York: Prentice-Hall, 1982.

Hickman, Craig R., and Michael A. Silva. *Creating Excellence.* New York: Plume Books/New American Library, 1984.

Hicks, Jerry, and Esther Hicks. *A New Beginning II.* San Antonio, Tex.: Abraham-Hicks Publications, 1995.

Holmes, Ernest. "Daily Guides to Richer Living." *Science of Mind* 69.10 (October 1996): 72.

Howard, David. "Playing a Supporting Role: An Interview with Paul Newman." *Hemispheres* (the magazine of United Airlines), October 1997: 24. Reprinted with permission.

Hunt, D. Trinidad. *Learning to Learn.* Kaneohe, Hawaii: Elan Enterprises, 1991.

———. *The Operator's Manual for Planet Earth.* New York: Hyperion, 1996.

Jordan, Sinda. *Inspired by Angels.* Nevada City, Calif.: Blue Dolphin Publishing, 1995.

Juline, Kathy. "A Return to Prayer: An Interview with Marianne Williamson." *Science of Mind* 69.9 (September 1996): 43.

Jung, Carl. *Man and His Symbols.* Mendocino, Calif.: Audio Scholar, 1994.

Kabat-Zinn, Jon. *Wherever You Go, There You Are.* New York: Hyperion, 1994.

Lancer, Bob. *Master Yourself, Master Your Life: An Introduction to the Wisdom of Natural Process and Conscious Living.* Phoenix, Ariz.: Limitless Light Publishing, 1984.

Lester, Joan Steinau. *Taking Charge: Every Woman's Action Guide to Personal, Political and Professional Success.* Berkeley, Calif.: Conari Press, 1996.

Liebig, James E. *Merchants of Vision*. San Francisco: Berrett-Koehler Publishers, 1994.

Lindbergh, Anne Morrow. *Gift from the Sea*. New York: Pantheon Books, 1975.

Luppi, Diana. *E.T. 101: The Cosmic Instruction Manual*. Santa Fe, N.M.: Intergalactic Council Publications, 1990.

Marciniak, Barbara. *Bringers of the Dawn: Teachings from the Pleiadians*. Santa Fe, N.M.: Bear & Co., 1994.

Markova, Dawna. *No Enemies Within*. Berkeley, Calif.: Conari Press, 1994.

McNamar, Linda. "Daily Guides to Richer Living." *Science of Mind* 69.9 (September 1996): 82.

McWilliams, Peter. *Life 101*. Los Angeles: Prelude Press, 1990.

———. *The Life 101 Quote Book*. Los Angeles: Prelude Press, 1996.

———. *Wealth 101*. Los Angeles: Prelude Press, 1992.

Moawad, Bob. *Whatever It Takes*. Edmonds, Wash.: Compendium, 1995.

Moorman, Chick. *Where the Heart Is: Stories of Home and Family*. Saginaw, Mich.: Personal Power Press, 1996.

Moyers, Bill. *The Power of Myth*. New York: Doubleday, 1988.

Muller, Wayne. *How, Then, Shall We Live?* New York: Bantam Books, 1996.

———. *Legacy of the Heart: The Spiritual Advantages of a Painful Childhood*. New York: Simon & Schuster, 1992.

Myss, Caroline. *Anatomy of the Spirit*. New York: Harmony Books, 1996.

———. *Spiritual Madness*. Boulder, Colo.: Sounds True Audio, 1997.

Nabokov, Peter. *Native American Testimony*. New York: Thomas Y. Corwell, 1978.

New Dimensions Journal. September/October 1997.

The New Jerusalem Bible. New York: Doubleday, 1985.

Oliver-Diaz, Philip, and Patricia A. O'Gorman. *Twelve Steps to Self-Parenting*. Deerfield Beach, Fla.: Health Communications, 1988.

Osborn, Carol. *How Would Confucius Ask for a Raise?* New York: William Morrow & Co., 1994.

Peale, Norman Vincent. *The Positive Principle Today*. New York: Wings Books, 1992.

Peck, M. Scott. *Further Along the Road Less Traveled*. New York: Simon & Schuster, 1993.

———. *The Road Less Traveled*. New York: Simon & Schuster, 1978.

Pendleton, Winston K. *Handbook of Inspirational and Motivational Stories, Anecdotes and Humor.* New York: Parker Publishing Co., 1982.

Piper, Watty. *The Little Engine That Could.* New York: Platt & Munk Publishers, 1990.

Ponder, Catherine. *The Dynamic Laws of Prosperity.* P.O. Drawer 1278, Palm Desert, Calif., 92261, 1985. Used by permission of the author.

———. *Open Your Mind to Receive.* P.O. Drawer 1278, Palm Desert, Calif., 92261, 1983. Used by permission of the author.

Prather, Hugh. *Notes to Myself.* Moab, Utah: Real People Press, 1970.

Proust, Marcel. *Aphorisms and Epigrams from Remembrances of Things Past.* Edited and translated by Justin O'Brien. New York: McGraw-Hill Paperbacks, Columbia University Press, 1948.

Rawson, Hugh, and Margaret Miner. *The New International Dictionary of Quotations.* New York: E. P. Dutton, 1986.

Rinpoche, Sogyal. *The Tibetan Book of Living and Dying.* San Francisco: Harper San Francisco, 1994.

Roberts, Kate Louise. *Hoyt's New Cyclopedia of Practical Quotations.* New York: Funk & Wagnall's, 1922.

Robinson, Jonathan. *Communication Miracles for Couples.* Berkeley, Calif.: Conari Press, 1997.

———. *The Little Book of Big Questions.* Berkeley, Calif.: Conari Press, 1995.

Roman, Sanaya, and Duane Packer. *Creating Money: Keys to Abundance.* Tiburon, Calif.: HJ Kramer, 1988.

Ross, Ruth. *Prospering Woman: A Complete Guide to Achieving the Full, Abundant Life.* Toronto: Bantam Books, 1982.

Safire, William, and Leonard Safire. *Words of Wisdom.* New York: Simon & Schuster, 1989.

Saint-Exupéry, Antoine de. *The Little Prince.* New York: Scholastic Book Services, 1971.

Salsbury, Glenna. *The Art of the Fresh Start.* Deerfield Beach, Fla.: Health Communications, 1995.

Saunders, Mary Chloe Schoolcraft. *Peace on the Wing.* Albuquerque, N.M.: Possibilities w/MCSS, 1997.

Sher, Barbara. *Wishcraft: How to Get What You Really Want.* New York: Ballantine Books, 1979.

Shigematsu, Soiku. *A Zen Harvest: Japanese Folk Zen Sayings.* San Francisco: North Point Press, 1988.

Simpson, James B. *Simpson's Contemporary Quotations.* Boston: Houghton-Mifflin Co., 1988.

Sinetar, Marsha. *Developing a Twenty-First Century Mind.* New York: Ballantine Books, 1991.

Singh, Tara. *Nothing Real Can Be Threatened.* Los Angeles: Life Action Press, 1989.

Steidl, Jeannine. *Lightbearer* 3 (April 1996): 1.

Toms, Michael. *At the Leading Edge.* New York: Larson Publications, 1991.

Tripp, Rhoda Thomas. *The International Thesaurus of Quotations.* New York: Perennial Library/Harper & Row, 1970.

Volkman, Arthur G. *Thoreau on Man and Nature.* Mt. Vernon, N.Y.: Peter Pauper Press, 1960.

Walsch, Neale Donald. *Conversations with God: An Uncommon Dialogue.* New York: Putnam, 1996.

Watts, Alan. *The Way of Zen.* New York: Vintage Books, 1957.

Wegscheider-Cruse, Sharon. *Choicemaking.* Deerfield Beach, Fla.: Health Communications, 1985.

Williams, Margery. *The Velveteen Rabbit or How Toys Become Real.* Philadelphia: Running Press, 1981.

Williamson, Marianne. *A Woman's Worth.* New York: Random House, 1993.

About the Authors

Jane Bluestein, Ph.D., is an internationally recognized educator, writer and speaker. An expert in the field of adult-child relationships, Jane's work includes a strong emphasis on self-care, self-acknowledgment and personal growth. She is a frequent guest expert on radio and television worldwide, and is the author of numerous books, including *Mentors, Masters and Mrs. MacGregor: Stories of Teachers Making a Difference; Parents, Teens and Boundaries* and *The Parent's Book of Lists: Dos and Don'ts of Effective Parenting.* Like her coauthors, Jane has spent much of her adult life on a personal and spiritual journey, and has regularly used journal-keeping as a tool for personal development since 1963.

Contact Dr. Bluestein for presentations, training and resources at Instructional Support Services, Inc., 1925 Juan Tabo NE, Suite B-249, Albuquerque, NM 87112-3359. Telephone: 800-688-1960 and 505-323-9044; fax: 505-323-9045; email: *jblue@wizrealm.com.* Visit Jane's Web site at http://www.janebluestein.com.

Judy Lawrence, M.S. Ed., is a financial counselor and a popular speaker on basic money management, with many years of experience helping people make the most of their money. As the author of the 100,000-copy bestseller *The Budget Kit: Common Cent$* and *The Money Tracker,* Judy has helped thousands nationwide take control of their finances in a practical, balanced and user-friendly way. She has been a featured guest on numerous television and radio shows, and has often been quoted and reviewed in national family and financial publications. Judy's personal journey includes a six-month, mid-career solo adventure through Africa and Europe to reflect upon and reassess her goals and priorities, which resulted in learning to appreciate each day and the unfolding of each moment.

Ms. Lawrence can be reached for consultation, presentations and resources at Common Cent$ Budgeting Corp., P.O. Box 13167, Albuquerque, NM 87192. Telephone: 800-283-4380 and 505-296-8792; fax: 505-296-0632; email: *judycents@aol.com.* Visit Judy's Web site at http://www.moneytracker.com.

SJ Sanchez, M.P.A., has worked in social services for over twenty years, in areas including health, mental health and education. She has worked as a stockbroker specializing in socially responsible investing and was recently integral to the formation of the largest family foundation in New Mexico, where she helped plot the course of future grantmaking for 200 to 300 nonprofit organizations. A native New Mexican and the eldest of seven children, SJ followed her undergraduate work in psychology with a master's degree in public administration, which she completed as a single mother of three children. She has lived and traveled throughout the world, and has been honored many times for her dedication to issues in the communities in which she has lived. Her recognitions include being selected for the National Hispana Leadership Institute in 1990.

Ms. Sanchez can be reached at 3401 Vassar NE, Albuquerque, NM 87107. Telephone: 505-244-0178; fax: 505-883-8495.

An HCI Bestseller

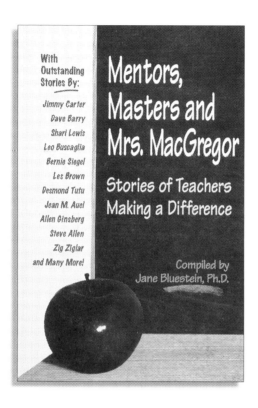

Mentors, Masters and Mrs. MacGregor
Stories of Teachers Making a Difference
Jane Bluestein, Ph.D.
This is a collection of inspiring stories about teachers and other special people who have made a positive and significant impact on our lives. Some stories are from famous people — Jimmy Carter, Dave Berry and Steve Allen — while others are ordinary folks with extraordinary stories.
Code 3375, 5 1/2 x 8 1/2, 260 pp., trade paper, $11.95

Bluestein on Family